W0381424

GO»
AHEAD

REALSCHULE BAYERN

9

Workbook
mit interaktiven Übungen

AUDIOS online

Deine **Audios** findest du auf scook.de/bayern. Dafür gibst du den unten stehenden Zugangscode in die Box ein.

scook

Deine **interaktiven Übungen** kannst du so freischalten:

1. Melde dich auf scook.de/bayern an. Beim ersten Besuch von scook.de/bayern musst du dich mit einer – nicht notwendig personifizierten – E-Mailadresse registrieren.
2. Gib den unten stehenden Zugangscode in die Box ein.
3. Damit deine Lernstandsdaten gespeichert werden, müssen du und deine Eltern uns bei der ersten Freischaltung der interaktiven Übungen eine Einwilligung dazu geben. Cornelsen speichert die Antworten deiner durchgeführten Übungen für die Nutzungsdauer der interaktiven Übungen. Für Volljährige (über 18 Jahren) ist das Einverständnis der Eltern nicht erforderlich.

Die Nutzungsdauer für die Online-Übungen beträgt nach Aktivierung des Zugangscodes zwei Jahre. In dieser Zeit speichern wir deine Lernstandsdaten für dich; nach Ablauf der Nutzungsdauer werden sie gelöscht.

Dein Zugangscode auf **www.scook.de/bayern**

vv2ek-exqnm

Cornelsen

INHALT

So viele Zeichen im Workbook – was bedeuten sie?

Die Ampel – Wie schwer fällt dir eine Übung?
In der Ampel kannst du markieren, wie schwer dir eine (Teil-)Übung gefallen ist: rot = schwer, gelb = mittel, grün = leicht.

Weiße und blaue Kreise – jeder so gut er kann
Leichtere Aufgaben sind mit einem leeren Kreis markiert und schwierigere mit einem vollen. Die Übungen ohne spezielle Markierungen sind auf einem Niveau, das alle Schülerinnen und Schüler lösen können.

Kopfhörer – Hörtexte online
14
Für dieses Angebot lädst du dir auf scook.de/bayern alle Tonaufnahmen im MP3-Format herunter. Den Zugangscode dafür findest du auf S. 1 deines Workbooks. Die Zahl unter dem Kopfhörer nennt dir die Track-Nummer, unter der du den entsprechenden Hörtext hören kannst.

Das Tablet weist auf Online-Aufgabenpakete hin.
Gehe dazu auf scook.de/bayern, gib deinen Zugangscode von S. 1 ein und wähle aus dem Inhaltsverzeichnis die passende Übungszahl.

Stift, Partner- und Gruppenarbeit – wie du diese Übungen bearbeiten sollst
Für Aufgaben, neben denen ein Stift abgebildet ist, schreibst du deine Antwort auf ein anderes Blatt Papier. Die beiden Köpfe beziehen sich auf Übungen, die du zu zweit bearbeiten kannst. Die drei Köpfe auf Übungen, die du in einer Gruppe bearbeitest.

Life in Australia

Unit 1

Words and pictures

1 Facts about Australia

Complete the sentences with information about Australia, using the correct form of the words in the box. There are two extra words.

camel • continent • coral • insect repellent • kangaroo • outback • parrot • rainforest • scuba-diving • sunscreen • Tasmanian devil

1 Australia is a ________________ you need to explore.

2 There are ________________ jumping around in the ________________.

3 You can see the ________________, a small but very loud and strong animal.

4 Mosquitos might bite you if you don't use ________________.

5 Beautiful ________________ fly around in the ________________.

6 You can go ________________ in the Great Barrier Reef.

7 ________________ looks like rock but is really an animal.

SB pp. 8-9

2 Outback survival

a **If you get lost in the outback, remember to STOP! What do you think the letters mean? For example: The 'O' stands for 'observe', which means to watch, look at and notice things. Circle the right answers. Then explain how each point can help you if you get lost.**

S sail – say – shake – shrug – sit ________________

T take – teach – think – trade – trip ________________

O observe – offer – open – own *to find something or somebody by listening and looking around*

P panic – plan – play – point – present ________________

b **Make a STOP safety poster. You can take the *Be sunsmart!* poster on SB p. 9 as an example.**

SB p. 9

First Australians

1 READING A history of injustice

Read the texts on SB pp. 10–11 again. One ending to each of the following sentences (1–4) is correct. Tick (✓) A, B, C or D.

1 The spirits from the Dreaming ...

- ☐ A are dead.
- ☐ B live on in people and sacred places.
- ☐ C are only part of the past.
- ☐ D are an important aspect of time.

2 The stolen generations ...

- ☐ A didn't get an apology for a long time.
- ☐ B got money from the government.
- ☐ C were taught their culture.
- ☐ D were taken by the first Europeans.

3 Valerie Linnow ...

- ☐ A met her mother later.
- ☐ B was allowed to see her two younger sisters.
- ☐ C was treated kindly by the women in the home.
- ☐ D was taken away from her brothers and six of her sisters.

4 Aboriginal and Torres Strait Islander people ...

- ☐ A came to Australia 20,000 years ago.
- ☐ B don't usually live in cities.
- ☐ C live longer than other Australians.
- ☐ D are less likely to have a job than other Australians.

SB pp. 10–11

2 Word families

The words in the middle belong to the same word families as words on SB p. 10. Find them and add them to the table. Then match each word (2–9) with its meaning. SB p. 10

1	identification (Ex. 1a)	*to identify*
2	to testify (Ex. 1a)	
3	fellowship (Text 2)	
4	integration (Text 2)	
5	upbringing (Text 2)	
6	apology (Text 2)	
7	communal (Text 3)	
8	indignant (Text 3)	
9	pride (Text 3)	

- the process of understanding or showing what somebody/something is ☐ *1*
- shared by people, especially those who live together ☐
- the way in which you are cared for and taught as a child ☐
- to make a statement, especially in court, that something happened or something is true ☐
- the act of bringing people together who were separated, because of colour, race, religion, etc. ☐
- the feeling that you respect yourself and expect others to respect you ☐
- to feel angry when something is unfair ☐
- what you say when you've done something wrong ☐
- a feeling of connection, for example in people who belong to the same group ☐

3 READING First Australians

Read these four texts about the first Australians and match them with the statements 1–6 below. Choose the correct text (A–D) and write its letter on the line. The texts may be chosen more than once. Then highlight the places in the text where you find the relevant information.

A People have lived in Australia for about 50,000 years. How they got there is still not clear. Australia has been an island since before there were people on earth. And there are no apes in Australia that they could have developed from. Did they come from southern Asia? If so, why and how did so many of them cross at least 120 kilometres of ocean to get to Australia? You need a lot of people to populate a new continent! European settlers first arrived in 1788. For tens of thousands of years before that, the Aboriginal people were there alone.

B When James Cook and his crew reached Australia in 1770, they were surprised that the indigenous people weren't very interested in them. As their ship sailed by, the Aboriginal people only looked at it for a moment and then returned to what they had been doing. They seemed to think about and see the world differently than Europeans. None of their languages had words for "yesterday" or "tomorrow"; they didn't build houses or own things. They seemed to live very peacefully: the land and the sea gave them everything they needed.

C Aboriginal and Torres Strait Islander people did not become Australian citizens until 1967. As activists point out, even dogs and cats were counted before Aboriginal people were. But although now citizens, many believe that the country's first people are still not treated equally. They experience many social and economic disadvantages. Although presently only 3% of the population is indigenous, they make up 27% of Australia's prisoners. But there is some good news. The indigenous population is increasing: by 2031 it might be greater than it was when the first colonists arrived in 1788.

D Uluru, the huge red rock that is one of Australia's most important landmarks, was not seen by European explorers until 1874. They called it Ayer's Rock, and from the late 1930s thousands of visitors came to see and climb it each year. Climbing Uluru, however, is not allowed by the laws of the Aboriginal Anangu people who are its traditional owners: the rock is sacred to them. In 1985, Uluru and its national park were given back to the Anangu community in an event called the Handback. In the 1990s, the Anangu put up signs asking visitors not to climb Uluru, but these signs were mostly ignored. In recent years, however, growing respect for and awareness of Aboriginal culture led to fewer climbers. The rock was permanently closed to climbers in October 2019.

1 More than a quarter of today's convicts are indigenous people. ☐

2 Aboriginal people recently stopped visitors from going onto one of their most important sites. ☐

3 European explorers had thought Australian natives would pay more attention to them. ☐

4 It is hard to explain how the first Australians came to the continent. ☐

5 There will soon be more Aboriginal Australians than there were before European settlers arrived. ☐

6 For about a hundred years, masses have travelled to one of Australia's most famous sights. ☐

SB pp. 10–11

Indigenous Australian art: past and present

1 REVISION Wandjina rock art

a Read the text. Then circle the correct form of each verb.

After the first Australians **(1)** *had arrived / were arriving* on the continent about 50,000 years ago, they **(2)** *began / had begun* making some of the world's oldest rock art. The huge Kimberley region in Western Australia has many examples of ancient rock art.

Wandjina is a traditional rock art form. There are examples of it that are about 5,000 years old in the Kimberley. The Mowanjum tribal groups believe that the Wandjina **(3)** *had created / created* the land and the people. Paintings of the Wandjina show figures that **(4)** *are are often looking like / often look like* ghosts or as if they are from space. When members of these tribes visit ancient paintings, they call out and say who they are and why they **(5)** *come / have come.*

It is very important to treat the sites respectfully. It is not okay to take photos with a painting in the background without permission or to take things from the caves. Even a stick lying on the ground may be important. It might **(6)** *be pointing / is pointing* to the painting sending a message. Even today, artists still **(7)** *paint / painting* the Wandjina. Millions of people around the world **(8)** *were watching / watched* the 2000 Olympics when a 12-metre-high Wandjina appeared at the opening ceremony. A Mowanjum artist **(9)** *had designed / was designing* it for the Games. Only people from Mowanjum tribes may paint the Wandjina. In 2011, a court decided it was illegal for other people to paint them after an artist **(10)** *had painted / was painting* the Wandjina and sold pictures of the figures.

b **Cho is telling Amy about the indigenous art she saw on her trip to Australia last year. Complete the dialogue by filling in the verbs in the correct tenses.**

Cho: While we **(1)** ____________ (visit) Australia last year we **(2)** ____________ (see) some cool rock paintings by Aboriginal artists.

Amy: Where was that? My family **(3)** ____________ (plan) a trip to Australia!

Cho: The Kimberley region in Western Australia. After my mother **(4)** ____________ (read) about the cool rock art there, she **(5)** ____________ (book) a trip with a tour group. An indigenous guide took us to the caves.

Amy: Why **(6)** ____________ (you/need) an indigenous guide?

Cho: Visitors **(7)** ____________ (not be allowed to) see all the paintings. Only men can see some and only women can see others. And only tribe members can see some.

Amy: **(8)** ____________ (you/have) any photos?

Cho: No, sorry. You're not allowed to take photos. While we were there, some other visitors **(9)** ____________ (take) photos and our guide **(10)** ____________ (tell) them to stop.

SB p. 12

2 Walkabout

a **Read the text. Then replace the simple past with *used to* where possible by underlining the verb and changing it to a form with *used to* on the right.**

Indigenous Australians sent teenage boys on "walkabouts" as a coming of age ritual. The boys walked miles into the wilderness where they survived on their own for several months.
Before the walkabout, the elders taught the boys how to survive alone in the wilderness. They also painted the boys' bodies and put decorations on them. Some tribes removed a tooth.
On walkabout, the boys sang traditional songs to ask the spirits for help. Following these "songlines" helped them to find their way through the wilderness. Walkabout wasn't a ritual for adults, but today people go on "walkabouts" to spend time alone and in nature. Today, the phrase "to go walkabout" is often used to describe people wandering away and not being responsible, for example "I don't know where Annie has been all week. She's gone walkabout."

used to send ______

b **What forms of art were used before and during a walkabout?**

______ ______ ______

SB p. 13

3 Changing times

Complete the sentences with *used to* or the simple past.

> You use *used to* for things that were true or often happened in the past, but not now. You can't use it for things/actions that only happened once: use the simple past instead.

1 Australia ______ (be) a British colony but now it's an independent country.
2 James Cook ______ (arrive) in Botany Bay in 1770.
3 There are wildfires in Australia every year, but they ______ (not be) as bad as they are these days.
4 Millions of animals ______ (die) in the Australian wildfires in 2020.
5 Aboriginal Australians ______ (not paint) their dot pictures on canvas.
6 Visitors ______ (be allowed to) climb Uluru, but the rules changed in 2019.

SB p. 13

Venomous creatures

1 MEDIATION Venomous snakes in Australia

Verwende die Informationen aus dem Text und bearbeite die Aufgaben (1–5) stichpunktartig auf Deutsch. Einzelwörter genügen nicht als Antwort.

Venomous snakes in Australia

The world's ten most venomous snakes all live in Australia. Visitors do not have to be very worried though. Most bites happen when a person is trying to hold or kill a snake. If you leave snakes alone, they will usually leave you alone. The development of antivenoms means that most snake bites do not kill their victims today. Some of their bites will, however, leave you screaming in terrible pain, so it is best to get out of their way. Below, you can find information about three of the most dangerous snakes.

Eastern brown snake

These nasty guys kill more people each year in Australia than any other snakes. Their venom is very dangerous and they often live in areas where there are lots of people. One was recently discovered in a Brisbane backyard.

Mainland tiger snake

Found on the south-east coast of Australia, mainland tiger snakes are responsible for many bites because they like to hunt mice in houses at night, where people sometimes step on them in the dark. Without antivenom, their bite can cause paralysis and even kill people.

Inland taipan

The shy taipan lives in dry, rocky areas, so you will not see them around cities. It is the most venomous snake on earth: its venom is at least fifty times more dangerous than that of any other snake.

Snake bites: Call 000 for emergency services immediately. Do not wash or suck the bite.

1 Gibt es in Australien besonders giftige Schlangen? (Um einen Aspekt ergänzen.)

____

____

2 Wie kommt es dazu, dass Menschen gebissen werden? (Zwei Situationen nennen.)

____

____

3 Was kann passieren, wenn man gebissen wird? (Drei Folgen nennen.) ______________

____

____

4 Welche Schlange ist am giftigsten und wo lebt sie? ______________

____

5 Wie verhält man sich am besten, wenn jemand gebissen wird? (Drei Aspekte nennen.)

____

____

SB p. 14

Having a conversation

1 LISTENING Conversations with Australians

01

a How would you react to what the people say? Listen and tick (✓) the right answer.

1
- Yes! ☐
- It is a nice day, isn't it? ☐
- Hi! ☐

2
- By train. ☐
- All right, thanks. ☐
- I'm going home. ☐

3
- No, I'm from Germany. ☐
- Yes, it's been a lot of fun! ☐
- I don't know. ☐

4
- They're terrible! ☐
- No, it sounds great! ☐
- I'm fine, thanks. ☐

5
- No, thank you. ☐
- Cereal and fruit. ☐
- The first meal of the day. ☐

6
- No worries. ☐
- Hello! ☐
- Cheers to you too! ☐

02

b Listen and check your answers.

SB p. 15

2 SPEAKING At a hostel

a You're visiting Australia and meet a friendly Australian at breakfast in a hostel. Complete your part of the conversation. Use the words given to form your questions and answers.

Aussie: G'day! Are there any free seats at your table?

You: ______________________________. (near/window)

Aussie: Thanks! I'm Drew. What's your name and where are you from?

You: ______________________________?

Aussie: I'm from Queensland, but I've always wanted to see Tasmania.

You: ______________________________? (sights/recommend)

Aussie: Well, the national parks are amazing. And Port Arthur is really interesting.

You: ______________________________?

Aussie: It's where they sent the worst convicts.
There's a scary old prison there.

You: ______________________________
______________________________?

Aussie: It takes about ninety minutes by car.
You can book a trip at the reception.

You: ______________________________!

b Act out the dialogue. Partner A plays the Australian. Partner B should not use the book: try to remember the answers you wrote. Then swap roles.

c Find a new partner. Look at page 55.

SB p. 15

Coast to Coast *(by David Fermer)*

1 **Australia's strict immigration laws**
Complete the text with the right words from the table below.

Australia's immigration (1) ____

Since 1992, Australia has put **(2)** ____ immigrants in **(3)** ____ . The law says that immigrants can be held there **(4)** ____ , although they can go back to their home country any time they want. Some of them have been there for many years. Many human rights organizations have **(5)** ____ conditions in the centres and **(6)** ____ changes to Australia's laws. Australia has **(7)** ____ some of the worst centres in recent years.

1	a politics	b policy	c police	d policing
2	a illegal	b unlegal	c illegally	d legal
3	a prisons	b welfare centres	c detention centres	d attention centres
4	a once	b at present	c for a while	d forever
5	a encouraged	b criticized	c realized	d ignored
6	a recommended	b denied	c recognized	d identified
7	a ridded	b get rid of	c got rid of	d get ridded of

SB pp. 16–18

2 WRITING **Asking for help**
Cooper and Kate from the story on SB pp. 16–18 contact organizations that they think could help Bashir. Write an email for them to Refugee Aid Australia. Include the following aspects:
- some facts about Bashir
- how and where you found him
- how you are helping him now
- ask for advice

Find a suitable beginning and ending. Write about 180 words. You need not write any addresses.

Writing an email to an organization
If you don't know the name of the person at an organization you are writing to, start your email with *Dear Sir or Madam*. Start the next line with a capital letter.
Use a polite, formal style. Make sure your email is well structured and that the purpose is clear.
End your email with *Yours faithfully*.
Your name goes on the next line.

SB pp. 16–18

Increasing your vocabulary

1 SPEAKING AND LISTENING Sports collocations

a Partner A: Look at page 55.
Partner B: Complete the questions with *do, go* or *play*. Use a dictionary if you need help.

1 What are two reasons why it's important to ________ sports?
2 Would you like to ________ yoga?
3 Do you ________ a team sport? If so, which one and why? If not, why not?
4 Which would you prefer to do: ________ jogging or hiking? Why?
5 Is it safe to ________ rugby? Why or why not?

03 b Listen and check.

c Ask your partner the questions from a as well as two more questions about sports. In your questions you should use *do, go* or *play*. Write down his or her answers. Report to the class.

d When do you use *do, go* and *play*? Write rules for each word. SB p. 20

2 LISTENING Learn idioms

04 a Listen to the statements. Use the context to decide what these sports idioms mean. Match each idiom (1–7) with its meaning (a–i). There are two meanings that you don't need.

1 the front runner	☐	a to be at a higher level than someone else
2 to be out of someone's league	☐	b to stop treating someone in a nice way
3 to drop the ball	☐	c someone who never does things the wrong way
4 to have a good innings	☐	d the person who seems most likely to win a race or competition
5 the gloves are off	☐	e by a little bit
6 to hit one out of the park	☐	f to fail at something you are responsible for
7 by a nose	☐	g by using your sense of smell
		h to have great success
		i to live for a long time

b Which sports are the idioms in a from? Discuss. Some idioms may be used in more than one sport.

American football • baseball • boxing • cricket • football/soccer • hockey • horse racing • running

SB p. 20

Describing sports

1 WRITING Physical education in Australian schools

a Choosing a topic: Look at the Australian school sports below. Which one sounds most interesting to you? Pick one to write about.

bushwalking

cricket

frisbee

netball

rock climbing

sailing

snorkelling

surfing

b Researching and organizing information: Do (online) research and fill in the information below. This will help you structure your text.

1 Name of the sport		2 Team sport ☐ Individual sport ☐
3 Where it is played/done		
4 Verbs for this sport:	5 Most important clothes/ equipment	6 Rules / Safety keywords

c Writing: Write a description of the sport you picked. Find a suitable beginning and ending. Use your notes from b and give each section a heading. Write about 180 words.

d Take turns reading each other one sentence about your sport. Try to guess which sport your partner is describing. If your partner can't guess, read another sentence. Don't say the name of the sport. After you have guessed each other's sport, swap partners. SB p. 21

1 Check your vocabulary

You can find the answers to these tasks on pages 61-62.

a Read the article and circle the correct words.

An Iranian writer who spent six years in an Australian **(1)** *detention centre / prison / community* on an island in Papua New Guinea has arrived in New Zealand. Behrouz Boochani was allowed to leave to accept a prize he won for a book he wrote by text messages. He says he will never **(2)** *bear / return / deny* to the country.

Boochani's book describes how he arrived on the island and his life there. He says that writing helped him to live through the **(3)** *authority / indignity / testimony* that the centre **(4)** *ignored / integrated / inflicted* on him.

Boochani left his home country for political reasons. He travelled to Indonesia, where he got on a boat to Australia with other refugees. The first boat broke and he nearly **(5)** *separated / drowned / drank*. The second boat arrived in Australian waters but was stopped: he and his **(6)** *fellow / regular / direct* passengers were sent to an Australian detention centre in Papua New Guinea.

b Complete the sentences by adding the correct prepositions or adverb to the verbs.

1 The Australian prime minister apologized ________ the stolen generations in 2008.

2 Thousands of Aboriginal families were broken ________ between 1910 and the 1970s.

3 Indigenous children suffered ________ being separated from their parents.

4 They were brought ________ in children's homes, where they were forced to soak ________ everything they were taught about a strange culture.

5 Parents weren't allowed to pass ________ their culture to their children.

6 Children were told to cut ________ the talk about their families.

7 Families used to dream ________ finding each other again.

2 Check your language

Complete Clementine's texts to her best friend from her holiday in Australia, using the correct present and past tenses.

Hello from the famous Bondi Beach! *We are surfing* (we / surf) here today! Soft sand, warm water, huge waves: ____________ (it / feel) like paradise! ____________ (I / book) a surfing lesson before ____________ (we / come) to Australia. I didn't want to miss the chance to experience this!

While ____________ (I / get ready) this morning, ____________ (I / find) a huge spider in my bag! ____________ (I / used to / be) scared of all spiders, but now I'm just scared of the Australian ones!

3 Check your mediation skills

You and your little brother find a special snail on the beach. Ask the lifeguard questions and tell your brother about the snail. Remember to be polite.

Brother: Wie heißt diese Schnecke? Und ist sie giftig?

You: ______________________________

Lifeguard: Oh, that's a cone snail[1]. Good that it's empty. They are dangerous if they are still alive! The ones you find in the water are very venomous. Don't pick them up ... or step on them!

You: ______________________________

____

Brother: Was passiert, wenn man gestochen wird?

You: ______________________________

Lifeguard: You have to go to hospital. There's no antivenom, but the doctors can help.

You: ______________________________

____

[1] **cone snail** Kegelschnecke

4 Check your speaking skills

a **It's your first day as an exchange student at your new school in Australia. Answer and ask questions.**

Teacher: Welcome to our class. Can you tell us a little about yourself?

You: ______________________________.

Student 1: Why did you want to spend a year in Australia?

You: ______________________________

______________________________.

Student 2: How did you learn to speak English?

You: ______________________________.

You: ______________________________?

Student 1: I've never been to Germany, but I'm learning German now.

You: ______________________________?

Student 2: This week we are playing soccer, but next week we'll start doing yoga.

You: ______________________________?

Teacher: You can sit at that empty desk near the window.

You: ______________________________.

b **Form groups of 4 and act out the dialogue.**

Spelling

You can find the answers to these tasks on pages 67-68.

05

1 LISTENING Understanding the spoken alphabet

Tick (✓) the letters you hear.

1	☐ D	☐ T	6	☐ Z	☐ C	11	☐ P	☐ B
2	☐ S	☐ X	7	☐ U	☐ Y	12	☐ E	☐ I
3	☐ A	☐ E	8	☐ J	☐ G	13	☐ S	☐ C
4	☐ K	☐ Q	9	☐ U	☐ W	14	☐ R	☐ A
5	☐ W	☐ V	10	☐ M	☐ N	15	☐ I	☐ Y

2 Spelling words

06

a Listen to the tour guide's voice message and write down the words and numbers he is spelling to you. Listen again if you need to.

	Name	City	Code
1			
2			
3			
4			

07

b Write down eight words from unit 1 you think will be hard for your partner to spell. Read each word to your partner: he or she should spell the word out loud. If you need help pronouncing the letters, you can listen to the alphabet or look at the guide on SB page 225.

3 SPEAKING A phone call

a Partner A: Look at page 56. Partner B: You are flying to Australia to take part in an exchange programme. Call the office of the exchange programme to get information about your trip and answer questions with the help of the prompts below. Partner A starts. Take notes.

2	Say hi, who you are (Alex Winter) and why you are calling (more information about trip).
4	Spell your first name and last name.
6	Ask what time your flight leaves.
8	Say thank you.
10	Give your email address (alex-winter@example.com) and ask the person politely to spell her/his name.
12	Agree and say the country code (49) and your phone number (0162 2082784).

Flight: ____________

Leaves at: ____________

Arrives: ____________

____

Spoke to: ____________

____

b Your partner should check your notes.

Charts and statistics

1 Numbers and statistics

Use the information given in the box and the table on the right to fill in the gaps.

1 The number of people in Australia:

in 1901: 4,000,000 in 2018: ______________

2 The median age of Australians was twenty-two point five in 1901. In 2018, it was

______________________________ .

3 In 1901, the ratio of males ______ females was 110 ______ 100. In 2018, the ratio of males ______________________ .

4 In 1901, thirty-seven ______________ per cent of Australians lived in a state capital.

In 2018, it was ________________________ or a little over ______________ .

Talking and writing about numbers, charts, graphs and statistics

Be careful with punctuation. English uses commas where German uses points and points where German uses commas.

- 18.2 % = eighteen point two per cent
- 986,000 = nine hundred and eighty-six thousand

Use the word *to* when speaking about ratios

- 6 boys : 4 girls = 6 boys to 4 girls

Fractions and parts:

- 50 % (per cent) / a half
- 25 % / a quarter
- 33.3 % / a third
- 75 % / three-quarters
- 66.6 % / two-thirds

Australian population		
	1901	2018
Population	4 million	25 million
Ø age	22.5 years	37.2 years
Gender ratio	110 m : 100 f	98 m : 100 f
% in capitals	37.2	67.1

Source: Based on ABS, Australian Demographic Statistics and Australian Historical Population Statistics

2 REVISION Talking about charts and diagrams

a Partner A: Look at page 56. Partner B: Use charts A and B to complete the questions below.

1 (A) ______________ Australian citizens were born in England?

2 (A) Where were 185,000 ______________ ______________________?

3 (B) What percentage of Australians belong to ______________?

4 (B) Which religion do a little more than (*fraction*) __________ of Australians belong to?

b Ask your partner for the missing information in the charts. Write the answers in the charts.

c Describe chart A to partner A.

- What kind of chart is it?
- What does it show?
- What is the most interesting information in the chart (e.g. highs and lows)?

A Top 5 countries of birth for people who have become Australian citizens

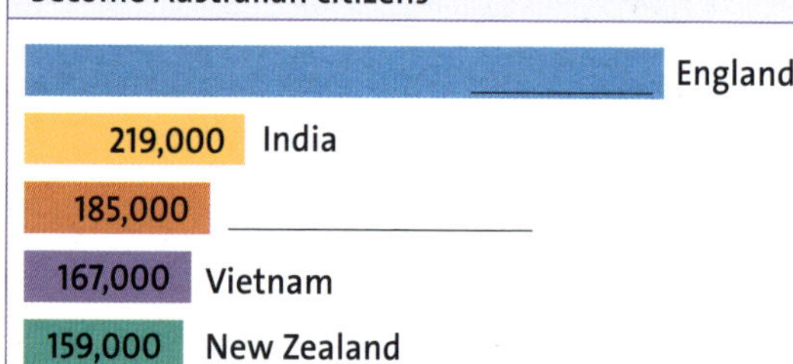

B Religion in Australia

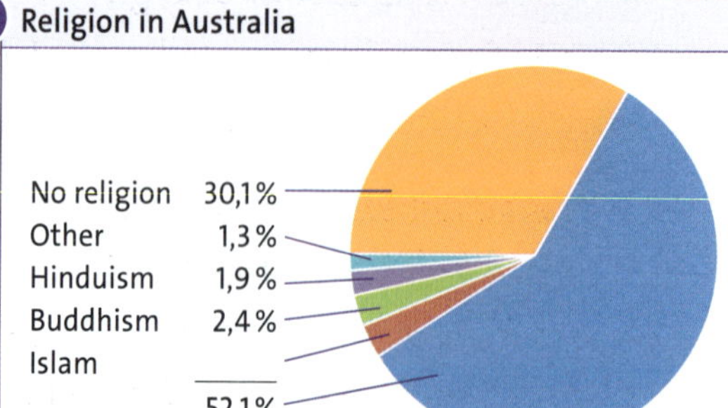

Source charts A and B: Based on ABS, Census of Population and Housing 2016

My world of work

Unit 2

Words and pictures

1 SPEAKING Part-time jobs

a Partner A: Look at page 57. Partner B: Hazel and Shevon are talking about their part-time jobs. Put Hazel's lines in the right places. There are three extra lines.

Hazel: ______________________________

Shevon: Yes, I work at the library, shelving books. But there's always time to read a little.

Hazel: Oh, that's cool! ______________________________

____

Shevon: I work three hours a day after school twice a week and four hours on Saturdays. Do you work?

Hazel: ______________________________

Shevon: What do you do?

Hazel: ______________________________ I dig holes, put the plants in, carry heavy bags ... but I like it!

Shevon: How much do you get an hour?

Hazel: ______________________________

Shevon: Not that much: only eleven dollars.

Hazel: ______________________________

Shevon: No, my parents say they'll pay for it.

Hazel: ______________________________, but my parents will pay the fees.

A lot of hard, dirty work! • Are you saving for college? • Do you have a part-time job? • Do you work every day? • How many hours a week do you work? • Yes, I have a job with a gardening company. • I'll need to pay my living expenses • Ten dollars. Do you get the same? • Twelve dollars. What does the library pay? • What's your part-time job?

08 b Listen to the dialogue and check your answers.

c Read the dialogue with your partner.

SB p. 25

2 MEDIATION The cost of college

A friend of yours is interested in studying in the US but doesn't know much about the cost. Answer your friend's questions in German, using information from SB p. 25.

1 Was kostet ein Studium an einer amerikanischen Universität? ______________________________

2 Das ist sehr viel Geld! Wie kann man das bezahlen, wenn die Eltern nicht so viel Geld haben? ______________________________

SB p. 25

Work and study abroad

09

1 LISTENING A summer abroad

a Alessio is calling the office of a language school. Listen and complete his notes.

Phone call with:	____________ *Experiences*
Courses with free places:	1 ____________ *in Australia*
	2 *Adventure classroom* ____________
Course in South Africa:	
Length:	____________
Ages:	*13–18-year-olds*
Tour along:	1 *Whale Route*
	2 ____________
Activities:	1 *see wild animals* ____________
	2 *go hiking*
	3 ____________ *or diving*
Learn English:	1 ____________ *all day (on the tour)*
	2 *an hour of lessons* ____________
Accommodation:	*in hostels,* ____________
Starting date:	____________
Further information via email:	1 *prices*
	2 *travel details including* ____________
	____________
	3 ____________

b Answer the following questions. You can listen to the conversation again if you need to.

1 Why does Alessio have time for a language programme this summer?

____

2 Why does Alessio have to call the office for information?

____

3 Why does Alessio think it will be easy for him to have roommates on the language course?

____

SB pp. 26–27

Expats in Germany

1 READING American Girl Scouts in Germany

a Read this profile of an American Girl Scout in Germany.

Mabel Sanchez was born in the USA, but her mother is from Bavaria and the family moved to Germany two years ago.
Luckily, there is an American Girl Scout troop in Mabel's town. There are troops in about 20 German cities, mostly where American soldiers used to be sent after World War II. Mabel has been a Girl Scout since kindergarten. Mabel grew up speaking German with her mother. She goes to a German school and mostly only speaks English at home with her father and brother. The Girl Scouts meet once every two weeks. This gives Mabel a chance to speak English with other girls.
A big part of Girl Scouts is learning to be a leader and developing new skills. Girls earn badges, take trips, explore the outdoors and do community service projects. Older girls help with the younger ones. The Senior Scouts can put these experiences and skills on their CVs. Mabel is one of the Seniors: girls who are in grades 9 and 10.
This year, the Seniors are earning their Community Service badges. Each girl has to volunteer for at least twenty hours with an organization, for example a food bank or an animal shelter. Mabel's troop is volunteering with a local children's hospital, making tie blankets.
The troop didn't have enough money to buy the material, so first the girls made cookies, brownies and muffins and sold them at sports events in town, earning about €350. The girls used the money to buy soft material in attractive colours and patterns. For each blanket, the girls cut two big pieces of material, one for the top and one for the bottom. After cutting around the edges, the girls tied the material.

The girls have made 25 blankets. They haven't taken them to the hospital yet: they're going to do that next week. The girls are going to give them to children there and stay to play games and read books. They're certain that the new blankets will be very welcome!

b What do the following words mean? Match the expressions (A–F) as used in the text with the correct definitions (1–8). Write the correct numbers in the table below. Be careful: there are two definitions that you do not need.

A used to
B experience
C bank
D attractive
E certain
F welcome

1 nice to look at
2 something that you have done or that has happened to you
3 (describing something) that happened regularly in the past but not now
4 convinced or sure
5 a statement about what you think will happen in the future
6 a place where something can be kept until it is ready to be used
7 something that a person does often
8 (describing something) that people are happy to get or have happen

A	B	C	D	E	F

c Underline at least three examples of the simple past (e.g. *she worked*) and circle the three examples of the present perfect (e.g. *she has worked*) in the text. SB pp. 28–29

2 REVISION At the hospital

The Girl Scouts have just arrived at the hospital. Complete their conversation with the nurse by using the simple past or present perfect. SB pp. 28–29

Nurse: (1) *Have you brought* ______ (you/bring) all the blankets with you?

Scout 1: No, (2) ______ (we/leave) some in the car. We couldn't carry them all!

Nurse: Where (3) ______ (you/buy) this material? It's so pretty!

Scout 1: (4) ______ (we/buy) it online.

Nurse: (5) ______ (you/read) this book to the kids before?

Scout 2: Yes, (6) ______ (I/read) it to them about ten times: it's their favourite!

Nurse: Who (7) ______ (I/talk) to on the phone?

Scout 2: (8) ______ (you/speak) to me.

Nurse: (9) ______ (you/ever/volunteer) before?

Scout 2: Yes, (10) ______ (we/volunteer) at the homeless shelter.

3 REVISION The next project

The Girl Scouts are planning their next volunteer project with their troop leader. Circle *will* or *be going to* to complete the text with the correct form. SB pp. 28–29

The girls **(1)** *are going to / will* help at a home for old people. They **(2)** *are going to / will* teach the people how to use smartphones and tablets. Each girl **(3)** *is going to / will* take a smartphone or a tablet with her. They **(4)** *are going to / will* go there on Tuesday. Some of the people who live there probably **(5)** *aren't going to / won't* be interested in learning how to use the devices. The girls **(6)** *are going to / will* speak loudly because some of the people don't hear well. They hope they **(7)** *are going to / will* be able to to go back again next week.

4 REVISION A presentation about Girl Scouts

Partner A: Look at page 57.

Partner B: You are preparing a presentation on Girl Scouts in Germany with your partner. Ask and answer questions about what you have learned so far with the help of the prompts below. You start.

1 Where and when • Girl Scouts • be founded?

4 Girl Scouts • be • in Germany • since 1946.

5 What other activities • Mabel's troop • do • in the next few months?

8 They • go camping • at a lake • in Southern Bavaria.

SB pp. 28–29

Your curriculum vitae in English

1 WRITING **Your CV**

You have found advertisements for three work experience places on a website: at a doctor's office, at a newspaper and at a bank. Choose one position and write your CV. Make sure it shows why you are the right person for the job.

SB p. 30

Name, address telephone, email

You can use the text you prepared on SB p. 30, 2b, but you may need to change it to emphasize aspects relevant to *this* position.

Put the dates on the left. Include volunteer work. If you still have a job, write the date you started and then *present*, for example *2021–present*.

List the schools you have been to. Put the dates on the left. Start with the most recent school. Then add training courses you have done.

Create categories like *Languages*, *Computer skills*, etc. relevant to *this* position.

www.example.net/online-cv

CURRICULUM VITAE

____

____

____

Personal statement F U K

____

____

____

____

____

Work experience

________	______________________
________	______________________
________	______________________
________	______________________
________	______________________

Education and training

________	______________________
________	______________________
________	______________________
________	______________________
________	______________________
________	______________________

Personal Skills

________	______________________
________	______________________
________	______________________
________	______________________

Cover letters

1 Summer camp job

a Girl Scout Mabel Sanchez is applying to work as a CIT (counselor[1]-in-training) at a camp in the US this summer. Read the job advert to find out what it is about.

b Circle information in the advert that Mabel can refer to in her cover letter, e.g. to emphasize relevant skills.

> www.example.net/happyhillsummercamp/jobs
>
> **Ready for your best summer ever?**
>
> Happy Hill Summer Camp is looking for fun-loving, hard-working teenagers (ages 13 to 15) who are interested in a leadership experience as CITs this summer. Spend your summer outdoors and develop your skills in camping, safety and working with younger campers. You'll learn how to develop and run a camp program while having a lot of fun and getting important skills for your résumé!
>
> Each day, you will spend about 2–3 hours leading younger campers in outdoor activities. For the rest of the day, you will take part in experiences with other CITs.
>
> To apply, please fill in the online registration form and upload your résumé and a cover letter. You will be asked to provide two references (including one from a teacher). Your contact person is Adam Lannert. Interviews (either in person or by video chat) will take place in April.

[1] **counselor** a person who leads a group of children at a summer camp

c Complete Mabel's cover letter. You may want to use information about her from pages 19–20.

Elchweg 12 92366 Hohenfels	← Applicant's address
______________________	← Name of the camp
______________________	← Contact person
______________________	← Date
______________________	← Greeting
______________________	← Introductory sentence
______________________	← Main paragraph
______________________	← Closing paragraph
______________________	← Closing sentence
______________________	← Closing greeting

SB p. 31

Formal phone calls

1 LISTENING AND SPEAKING Arranging a video interview

10

a Adam Lannert from Happy Hill Summer Camp is calling Mabel to make an appointment for a video interview for a position as a CIT (counselor-in-training). Listen to their conversation and complete Mabel's notes.

Call from Adam Lannert *April 3rd*

Received my (1) __________, *called to* (2) __________ *a video interview*

Date/Time: (3) __________

Will send link for (4) __________ *before* (5) __________

Interviewers: (6) __________, (7) __________,

(8) __________

Length: (9) __________

Want to hear about (10) __________, (11) __________

b Act out the phone call with a partner. Use your notes from a for help. SB p. 32

2 Business English

Joshua is calling Happy Hill for more information about the CIT positions. Read his conversation with Adam Lannert. Use the words in the box to make Joshua's statements more formal.

advertisement • attend • certain • child care • few • goodbye • hello • punctual • thank you • yes

Adam: Happy Hill Summer Camp. This is Adam Lannert.

Joshua: (1) Hi. My name is Joshua Martin and I saw your (2) ad for CITs. I have a (3) couple of questions.

Adam: I'm happy to help. What would you like to know?

Joshua: I saw that there's a training course the week before camp. Do all of the CITs have to (4) go for the whole week?

Adam: Yes, all CITS are required to take part every day from 8 am until 3 pm.

Joshua: I'm not (5) sure I could be (6) on time: I have to do chores at home in the morning. I'll talk to my parents about it.

Adam: Good idea. Do you have any other questions?

Joshua: (7) Yeah. Do CITs have to have experience of (8) babysitting?

Adam: Well, it's great if they do, but it's not required.

Joshua: (9) Thanks for your time.

Adam: You're welcome. Goodbye.

Joshua: (10) Bye.

1 __________
2 __________
3 __________
4 __________
5 __________
6 __________
7 __________
8 __________
9 __________
10 __________

SB p. 32

3 SPEAKING Making formal phone calls

Partner A: Look at page 58. Partner B: Look at page 59.

The fun they had *(by Isaac Asimov)*

1 The world in 2155

Use the following words from the story SB pp. 33–35 to make predictions about the year 2155.

Example: *waste* Everything will be recycled: there will be no more *waste*.

1 *ugly* ______________________

2 *mechanical* ______________________

3 *(to) calculate* ______________________

4 *(to) adjust* ______________________

5 *(to) light up* ______________________

SB pp. 33–35

2 READING In the story

a For each question, tick (✔) the correct answer.

1 Why did Margie write about the book in her diary?

A The subject of the book was extremely exciting. ☐
B She wasn't used to seeing books in that form. ☐
C The book wasn't for children. ☐
D The book was on a screen. ☐

2 How do the children complete homework and tests?

A They use a punch code. ☐
B They tap a screen. ☐
C They record voice messages. ☐
D They write them with paper and a pencil. ☐

3 How does Tommy feel about Margie?

A He thinks she knows a lot for her age. ☐
B He feels superior to her. ☐
C He's interested in hearing her opinions. ☐
D He appreciates her company. ☐

4 How does Margie feel during school?

A She can concentrate better without other children. ☐
B She likes having her mother in the house. ☐
C She is often sad. ☐
D She feels lonely. ☐

b What would Margie say? Circle the correct answer.

A Reading books on paper is a lot better than reading them on a screen.

B My father knows nearly as much as the mechanical teacher.

C Learning fractions is easier than learning geography.

D I don't like getting marks from the mechanical teacher.

SB pp. 33–35

3 SPEAKING Supporters and challengers

a Make groups of three.
Partner A: You agree with the statement below. Write down three arguments in support of it.
Partner B: You disagree with the statement below. Write down three arguments against it.
Partner C: Do you agree or disagree with the statement below? Write down your reasons.

> Replacing teachers with computers is a good idea.

1 ______________________________

2 ______________________________

3 ______________________________

b Partner A and B: Discuss your arguments for two minutes. The phrases on the right may help you.
Partner C: Listen to A's and B's arguments. Decide which arguments are better and explain your decision in class. You can use the reasons you wrote down in a.

> I believe/feel/find/think ...
> In my opinion/view, ...
> If you ask me, ...
> I agree with you. / I think so too.
> You've got a good point there, but ...
> I don't agree with you about ...
> I'm not sure that's true.

c You can swap roles and do the activity again using the following statements.

> Teaching children at home is better than sending them to school.
> Ebooks are superior to books on paper.

SB pp. 33-35

4 LISTENING Predictions for the future

11

You will hear five statements by experts on the future. Which of the topics below do they make predictions about? Write the correct numbers (1–5) in the boxes next to the categories (A–H). Use each number only once. (You will have 5 seconds after the first listening and five seconds after the second listening.)

A Education	☐	E Communication	☐
B Employment	☐	F Housing	☐
C Transport	☐	G Climate	☐
D Health	☐	H Politics	☐

SB pp. 33-35

5 WRITING Guided writing

Continue Margie's diary entry. Include the following aspects:

- if she prefers books on paper or on a screen
- what she did after school
- a description of one interesting aspect of her life in the future

Margie's diary entry starts like this: *Today Tommy found a real book!*
Write about 170 words.

SB pp. 33-35

Talk about work

1 SPEAKING **Working conditions**

Partner A: Look at page 58. Partner B: Look at page 59.

2 MEDIATION **About jobs**

You're on holiday with your parents in the US. A friendly woman in a museum café starts a conversation. Your parents speak more French than English, so you interpret for them.

Woman: Hi there! How're you doing today? That sounds like German you're speaking. Is that right?

You: Hello! Yes, we're from Germany.

Woman: I thought so! I've seen so many German tourists today! It seems like you have a lot of vacation time. How many days do you get a year?

Father: Was möchte sie wissen?

You: ______________________________

Father: Wir bekommen dreißig Tage im Jahr.

You: ______________________________

Woman: That many? That's amazing. Most Americans only get 15 or 20 days a year.

You: ______________________________

____

Mother: Wie viele Stunden arbeitet man pro Woche?

You: ______________________________

Woman: Well, it's different in each company. In a full-time job, you work about forty hours a week. How about in Germany?

You: ______________________________

____

Father: Bei uns ist es so ähnlich, vielleicht ein bisschen weniger: eher 38 oder 39 Stunden pro Woche.

You: ______________________________

Mother: Haben Sie hier auch flexible Arbeitszeiten?

You: ______________________________

Woman: Well, you usually can be more flexible if you're self-employed, of course. And it depends on the job. But a lot of companies are trying to offer more flexible hours.

You: ______________________________

____

SB p. 36

1 Check your vocabulary

You can find the answers to these tasks on pages 62–63.

a Match the adjectives (a–k) with the correct descriptions (1–9). There are two extra words.

Someone who ...

1 comes and does things on time is ... ☐
2 tells the truth and doesn't steal is ... ☐
3 does things with and for people to make it easier for them is ... ☐
4 acts in a way that is open and kind is ... ☐
5 waits without being annoyed is ... ☐
6 is able to produce something new, especially art, is ... ☐
7 is good at planning and keeping things tidy and available is ... ☐
8 does what he/she is supposed to do is ... ☐
9 behaves politely to people, especially people like parents, teachers and bosses, is ... ☐

a attractive
b helpful
c honest
d organized
e patient
f flexible
g respectful
h responsible
i friendly
j punctual
k creative

b Number the steps of getting a job in the right order (1–6).

☐ a Write a cover letter
☐ b Arrange an interview
☐ c Send your application
☐ d Attend the interview
☐ e Read a job advertisement
☐ f Write a thank-you note to the interviewer

2 Check your language

Complete the answers to the interview questions, using the present perfect, simple past and future (*will* or *going to*).

Q: Why have you applied for this job?
A: I **(1)** ____________ (see) the advert and **(2)** ____________ (think) I would be perfect for the position.
Q: Had you already heard of our company?
A: Yes, I **(3)** ____________ (use) your products for years.
Q: Have you ever had a difficult boss?
A: No, I **(4)** ____________ (be) lucky: they **(5)** ____________ (be) very easy to work for!
Q: What are you going to do after you leave school?
A: I **(6)** ____________ (travel) around the US this summer. In autumn I **(7)** ____________ (probably start) an apprenticeship.
Q: Where do you think you'll be in five years?
A: I hope I **(8)** ____________ (have) a job in a bank.

3 Check your speaking

a You are calling an English man in your town to apply for a job as a dog walker. Write suitable phrases.

Man: Hello?

You: ______________________________

Introduce yourself and say why you are calling.

Man: Oh, wonderful. Do you have experience of dog walking?

You: ______________________________

____

Say yes and tell him a little about it.

Man: That sounds perfect. C&#?d !$u *$m/ f&r an §?#erv*%w on Tuesday &# &#?! &#?

You: ______________________________

Tell him politely that you couldn't hear that.

Man: Could you come for an interview on Tuesday at 6 pm?

You: ______________________________

Tell him that you don't have time on Tuesday and why.

Man: What about Wednesday at 4 pm?

You: ______________________________

Agree to this time. Thank him.

Man: You're welcome. I'll see you then.

You: ______________________________

End the call politely.

b Act out the dialogue with a partner. Take turns playing the two roles.

4 Check your writing

Write headings for the following items in a CV.

______________	2019 – present Figgleston Secondary School
______________	2019 Completed volunteer art teacher training, Figgleston library
______________	2021 – present Volunteer art teacher, Figgleston library
______________	As a very creative person, I'm looking for a position ...
______________	Microsoft Word, Microsoft PowerPoint, photo editing
______________	Planning activities for large groups ...
______________	Presenting, demonstrating and explaining activities ...
______________	First languages: English and French; Foreign language: Spanish

The digital age

Unit 3

Words and pictures

1 SPEAKING **iRony**

The picture from the video shows a game where you use letters to make words on a board. Here, the players have put down slang words. Discuss: What is the link between the picture and the quote? How true/effective is the quote? Does it help that it rhymes? Think of examples to support your opinion.

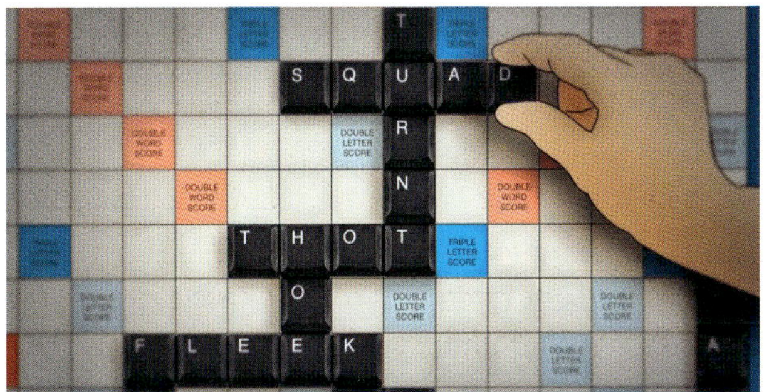

Twitter kills prose[1] in 140 letters
Language devolves[2] while technology betters.

[1] **prose** writing that is not a poem [2] **to devolve** to become worse

SB pp. 42–43

2 Playing a word game

a Look at the seven letters. How many words (2–7 letters) can you make from them in five minutes? Write them down below. Check your words in a dictionary if you need to.

T 1 | B 3 | R 1 | E 1 | H 3 | A 1 | D 2

b Compare with a partner. Who found more words? Add up the points (given next to each letter) to find out who has the word with the highest score.

SB pp. 42–43

3 WRITING **Writing rhymes**

a Write down one rhyme word for each of these words.

1 blue ______ 3 say ______ 5 you ______

2 sign ______ 4 ache ______ 6 cold ______

b Write two lines that rhyme (like the quote from ex. 1) about digital media. You can use words from a.

c Find or draw a picture to go with your rhyme. You can find pictures in magazines, use Creative Commons pictures from the internet, etc.

SB pp. 42–43

Logging off

1 REVISION How German teens use media

Use information from the graph to match the sentence parts about German teens and media below.

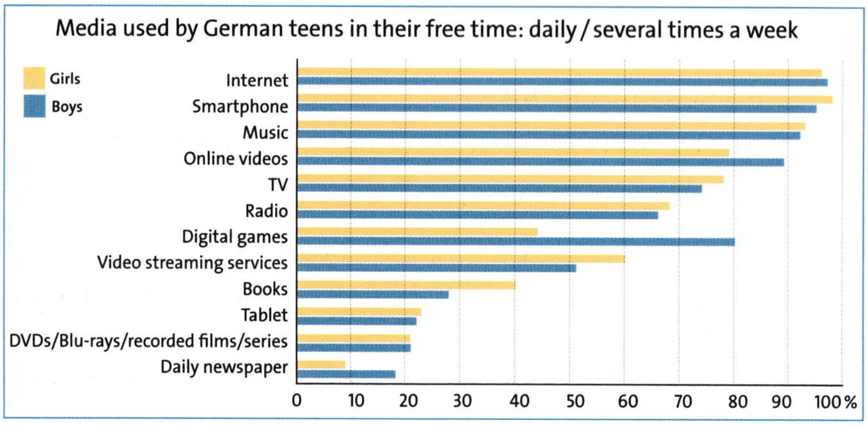

Source: JIM 2019

1 Nearly all German teens use the internet and a smartphone [d]
2 Girls and boys use the internet, smartphone and music [ ]
3 Less than half of German teens read a book [ ]
4 Girls read books [ ]
5 Girls play digital games [ ]
6 The chart doesn't tell you how media use has changed [ ]
7 It also doesn't tell you how long teens use media [ ]

a more than once a week.
b more often than boys.
c over the years.
d several times a week or every day.
e about half as much as boys do.
f every day.
g in about the same numbers.

SB pp. 44–45

2 WRITING Rules for digital media use

a Cristal is tired of spending so much time online, so she's made some rules for herself. Read her rules. Write down if they would help you reduce your screen time and why.

1 Schedule online time: only go online at these times.
2 One screen-free day each week.
3 Don't use phone in bed.

Rule 1 would/wouldn't help me because ______________________

____

Rule 2 ______________________

____

Rule 3 ______________________

____

b Make three more rules for yourself. Then compare with a partner.

SB pp. 44–45

Online issues

1 Interviewing an influencer

a **You've interviewed Sophie Zuggs, a famous fashion influencer. While writing your article, put these quotes into reported speech.**

1 "I can't believe how many followers I have." • **2** "I never expected to attract so many followers." • **3** "I've been really lucky: I've had a lot of good advice." • **4** "My sister is helping me to write a new book." • **5** "I tried to write it by myself, but it is too much work." • **6** "Ali is going to be in my next video." • **7** "We'll give away 500 free copies of the book in September."

Interview with Sophie Zuggs

With more than 10 million followers, Sophie Zuggs is one of today's most popular internet stars. In an interview, she told me that **(1)** ______________________ and that **(2)** ______________________. She said that **(3)** ______________________.

These days, Sophie has a new project. She told me that **(4)** ______________________. She said that **(5)** ______________________.

Apparently, her sister Ali will also get in front of the camera. Sophie said that **(6)** ______________________. Will Ali be the next big influencer?

For those of you who can't wait to read the book: Sophie said **(7)** ______________________.

b **During your interview last month, Sophie told you about some of her other activities. Read the quotes in the box and check the article below for mistakes in tense forms and time words. Underline the mistakes and correct them on the right.**

"We're going to open an online shop next month." • "I was ill last week, so I didn't post very much." • "I'm still not feeling very well this week." • "A photographer is coming to take my photo for the cover of the book tomorrow."

Sophie said that they are going to open	*were going*
an online shop next month. She told me	______
that she was ill last week,	______
so she didn't post very much. Sophie	______
also said that she still isn't feeling	______
very well this week. She added that	______
a photographer is coming to take her	______
photo for the cover of the book tomorrow.	______

c Your friend wants to know what you asked Sophie Zuggs. Use your notes to tell him.

1 I asked her how she ______________________.

2 I wanted to know how ______________________

______________________.

3 I also asked her ______________________

______________________.

4 And I wanted ______________________

______________________.

5 ______________________.

6 ______________________

______________________.

7 ______________________

______________________.

1. *How are you doing today?*
2. *How do you feel about your success?*
3. *Why do you think you've been so successful?*
4. *What new projects are you working on?*
5. *Does anyone help you with your work?*
6. *Is there anything you don't enjoy about being famous?*
7. *What tips can you give people who want to become influencers?*

SB pp. 46–48

2 Becoming an influencer

What tips did Sophie Zuggs have for people who want to become influencers? Rewrite the quotes for your article, using *asked, told* and *advised*.

1 Please be careful with what you share about yourself. ______________________.

2 Don't post anything negative about other people. ______________________.

3 Don't copy other people. ______________________.

4 You should find something that makes you special. ______________________.

5 You shouldn't expect to become a star overnight. ______________________.

6 Please don't take it personally if you get negative comments from jealous people. ______________________.

SB p. 48

Announcements

12 **1** LISTENING **Getting the details**

You will hear the recording twice. For each question, tick (✔) the correct answer.

1 What will happen at 10:00?

A ☐

B ☐

C ☐

2 What will the weather be like later today in New York?

A ☐

B ☐

C ☐

3 Which product is 50 % cheaper?

A ☐

B ☐

C ☐

4 How can you get around the park quickly?

A ☐

B ☐

C ☐

5 What should you do now if you want to go to the 44th street station?

A ☐

B ☐

C ☐

6 What will be on the music news later about the band Ugly Diary?

A ☐

B ☐

C ☐

7 What can you do at the library on Wednesday this week?

A ☐

B ☐

C ☐

SB p. 49

13 **2 LISTENING Media diary project**

You will hear some information about a media diary project at school.
Fill in missing information.

SB p. 49

Media diary project

Where to write the diaries: **(1)** ______________________

Website with examples of diaries: **(2)** www.example.com______________________

How long to keep the diaries: **(3)** ______________________

Date when diaries need to be completed: **(4)** ______________________

Not necessary to write **(5)** ______________________ of people we use media with

Data should be given in the form of a **(6)** ______________________

The boy who harnessed the wind
(by William Kamkwamba and Bryan Mealer)

1 READING AND WRITING **Harnessing the wind**

Each picture shows a step in putting up the windmill. Write a caption for each picture, using quotes from the text on SB pp. 50–52. You may need to leave out or change words to make captions that are as short and clear as possible.

1 *I put the wire over the top rung of the ladder, then dropped it down to Gilbert.*

2 ______________________________ .

3 ______________________________ .

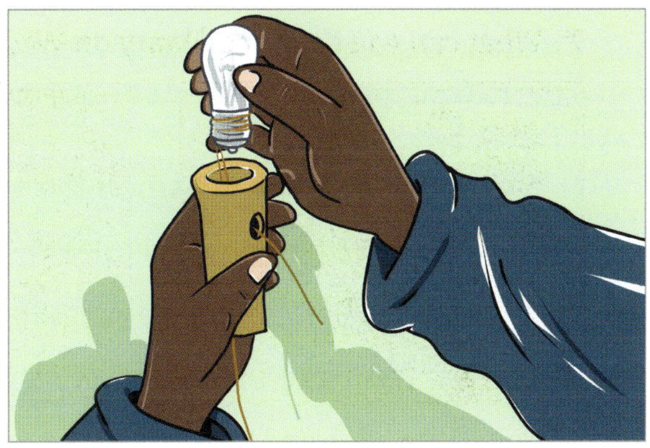

4 ______________________________ .

5 ______________________________ .

6 ______________________________ .

SB pp. 50–52

2 USE OF ENGLISH Words from the story

a These sentences are wrong. Replace one word or a two-word phrase in each sentence. Underline the wrong word(s) and write the correct word(s) on the lines.

1 The boys all worked hard to get the windmill down the tower. ____________

2 William had a monthly school fee of 80 dollars. ____________

3 When the windmill was far from the tower Gilbert tied it down. ____________

4 William made a socket out of a piece of wood. ____________

5 William put a long copper wire around the top of the bulb. ____________

6 The villagers said it would be possible to make electricity from the wind. ____________

7 The villagers believed William until they saw the bulb light up. ____________

b Read each sentence. Which of the words below it could you use to replace the underlined word without changing the meaning of the sentence? Circle the correct word(s). There may be more than one word you could use.

> What does the underlined word or phrase mean? The words below the sentence may make sense in the sentence, but do they really have a similar meaning? You can look them up in the back of the book (SB pp. 181–222) or in a dictionary to check.

1 William found a way to harness the wind.
connect use join stop control enjoy ride change slow

2 Geoffrey stood on the middle rungs to guide the machine as it went up.
direct watch touch organize hold stop steer follow

3 'You do your job and I'll do mine,' he replied.
ordered asked told me whispered shouted answered said

4 Geoffrey joined me at the top of the tower to secure the windmill in place.
see put hold attach push pull grab take follow

5 Within a few minutes, ...
In In just After Before During While

6 ... there were a dozen people at the base of the tower.
a lot of twelve a few a million a couple of many interested

7 There were about thirty adults, and just as many children.
even more just thirteen exactly the same number of fewer

8 My heart nearly burst.
exploded broke opened sang filled jumped beat

c Write the synonyms from b in your vocabulary book.

SB pp. 50–52

An ad for a home assistant

1 MEDIATION **Stevie Look**

a Read the advert for the Stevie Look home assistant.

Stevie Look 6

Stevie Look lets you take a look at the world!
A beautiful seven-inch screen adds images to Stevie's many offerings. Stevie Look can show you videos, TV shows, movies and the news. You can also use Stevie to listen to music, radio stations, audiobooks and podcasts.
You can make video calls with contacts who also have a Stevie Look. People can also connect to you with a computer, smartphone or tablet. And, of course, you can use Stevie Look to talk to people through other Stevie devices in your home.
Stevie Look lets you easily control your smart home. See who's at the front door with a connected security camera. View your temperature controls and light settings.
You can easily personalize your homescreen: give it a high-tech look or use it to show you relaxing pictures. You can also program Stevie Look to use your photos as its background.
Imagine cooking a meal with Stevie Look showing you every step of the recipe. Or having your to-do list in front of your eyes as soon as you ask to see it. Take a quick look at the weather and traffic while you're on your way out the door.
With Stevie Look, you never need to worry about privacy. A large switch will quickly show you whether the camera and microphone are on or off.
Setting up your Look Nothing could be easier! Just plug it in and follow the simple directions on the screen to connect to your Wi-Fi network. Finished!

b **Compare the advert in a with the one on SB p. 53. Write down the main difference between Stevie and Stevie Look.** ______

c **Verwende die Informationen aus dem Text in a. Bearbeite die Aufgaben (1–5) stichpunktartig auf Deutsch. Es ist keine wörtliche Übersetzung nötig, die Aspekte müssen inhaltlich jedoch vollständig erfasst sein. Einzelwörter genügen nicht als Antwort.**

1 Mit welchen Geräten kann man dich per Stevie Look erreichen? ______

______

2 Wie kann das Gerät zur Sicherheit im Haus beitragen? ______

______

3 Welche Einstellungen im Haus kann man mit dem Stevie Look steuern (2 Details)? ______

______

4 Wie kann man seine Privatsphäre schützen? ______

______

5 Wie richtet man das Gerät ein? ______

______

SB p. 53

Evaluating adverts

1 Talking about adverts

Tick (✓) one correct answer to each question. How can you talk about …

SB p. 54

1 … what the advert tries to do?	☐ The aim of the ad is to …	☐ The advert will …	☐ The advert wants to …
2 … a person in the advert?	☐ The star of the advert is …	☐ The figure in the advert is …	☐ The model in the advert is …
3 … a noticeable feature of the advert?	☐ It grabs your attention through …	☐ The … in the advert grabs your eyes.	☐ My opinion of the advert is …
4 … what is missing in the advert?	☐ It addresses concerns …	☐ The advert lacks …	☐ The language is …
5 … people who will like the advert?	☐ This ad will appeal to …	☐ The ad shows people who …	☐ I like how the advert …
6 … what the advert communicates?	☐ The advert gives contact information for the company …	☐ The message of this advert is …	☐ There aren't any people communicating in this advert …

2 Cool Colours

Talk to a partner about the advert on the right. Discuss the aspects below. Some information is given directly in the advert; some information requires your personal evaluation of the advert.

product name • type of product • slogan • target audience • lifestyle • key words • advert design • how to use the product • type of advert (TV, magazine, social media, …)

That's interesting. You think that this ad's target audience is …, but I thought it will appeal to …

I don't think that you would see this advert in/on … I would expect to see it …

Why do you think that … is a key word in the advert? I thought … and … were key words.

SB p. 54

1 Check your vocabulary

You can find the answers to these tasks on pages 64–65.

a Use the word given in capitals at the end of the lines to form a word of the same word family that fits in the space in the same line.

1 Eric is always careful about ____________ his computer when he's finished using it. (LOG)
2 We prefer ____________ movies and shows to watching them on TV. (STREAM)
3 She ____________ down to read the comments after she finished the article. (SCROLL)
4 Somebody guessed my ____________ (PASS) and ____________ into my account. (HACKER)
5 Turn off all of your ____________ devices until the plane has landed. (ELECTRICITY)
6 Try ____________ your device if it's not working correctly. (SET)
7 You can do that by ____________ the button on the side of the device. (PRESSURE)
8 She updates her ____________ every couple of hours, but I hardly ever do that. (STATE)

b Write the missing words and definitions.

1 ____________________________	50 % off
2 During one of these, a store sells things for less money than the usual price.	____________
3 ____________________________	warranty
4 ____________________________	to consume
5 A large shop is made up of several of these, each selling a different kind of things.	____________

2 Check your language

14

a Your friend Andy left you a voice message to tell you about his party. Listen and take notes.

b Complete the dialogue with your friend Artea, using reported speech and your notes from a.

You: Andy called me last night. He was talking about (1) ____________________.
Artea: Did he say when we should be there?
You: He said (2) ____________________. He (3) ____________________ on time. And he asked me (4) ____________________.
Artea: My mum said she'd pick us up at 11 pm. Did he say anything about food and drinks?
You: Yes. He said (5) ____________________ a lot of food (6) ____________________ and that Sterling (7) ____________________.
Artea: Did he tell you how many people are coming?
You: He said (8) ____________________ ten friends. And he asked me (9) ____________________ the party.

3 Check your mediation skills

Your grandmother's new smart light bulb only came with directions in English. She's sent you a picture of the directions. Tell her on the phone in German how to set it up.

You: Hast du die App schon installiert? Und ist die Birne schon in der Lampe?

Oma: Ja.

You: Prima. Nun Schritt 2: ____________________

Und Schritt 3: ____________________

____

Oma: Mache ich. Und nun?

You: ____________________

Und dann im Menü links auf das Wort „Light".

Oma: OK.

You: Ich hatte für dich ja bereits ein Smart&Bright-Konto eingerichtet. ____________________

Oma: Moment ... Ja, es hat geklappt.

You: Super. ____________________ auf dem Bildschirm erschienen?

Oma: Ja!

You: ____________________ Jetzt kannst du die Birne über die App steuern: ____________________

Oma: Vielen Dank!

Set up your new smart light bulb in seven easy steps.

Step 1 Install the Smart&Bright app on your phone.

Step 2 Turn on the device.

Step 3 Open the app. Click on the Home symbol at the bottom of the screen.

Step 4 Click on the + symbol at the top of the screen.

Step 5 On the menu on the left, click on the type of device (Light) you want to install.

Step 6 Log into your existing Smart&Bright account or set one up quickly and easily.

Step 7 Your new bulb will appear on the screen. Click on it. You can now control the light bulb with the app. You can turn it off and on and even change the colour!

4 Check your listening skills

15

Look at the advert. Then listen to the dialogue and complete the sentences.

Rob: I think I'll get a pair of these jeans. I like the advert. The ____________________ and ____________________ the jeans are just comfortable and easy.

Nell: ____________________ who want basic clothes, not luxury.

Rob: Right, that's what I like. And the advert ____________________: it says that the jeans are made from organic cotton.

Nell: I think that you're exactly ____________________!

Like hanging out with your best friends.

That's what a pair of **Cut Jeans** feels like. Comfy, fun and free.

Organic cotton makes you feel good about the environment too.

Speaking

1 **SPEAKING** **Older people and modern communication devices**

a **Partner A: Look at page 60. Partner B: Talk to Partner A. Speak for about three minutes.**

1 Describe each photo. Look at SF 10 SB p. 133 for help.
Describe the people and places, objects, positions, activities and weather.

In the photo on the left there are ... They're ...

2 Compare and contrast the situations shown in the photos.
Compare: How are the people/objects/situations similar?
Contrast: How are they different?

The people in both photos are ... In the photo on the right the woman is ..., but in the other photo there are ...

3 How can modern communication devices bring younger and older people together?
Use the photos to develop your ideas. How are younger and older people coming together here? Can you think of other ways?

Younger people can ... Older people can use ... to ...

b **Give your book to partner A, so s/he can fill in the feedback form for you.**

You ...	☺ ☺ ☺	*Notes: What was especially good? What could be better?*
spoke clearly and in a good speed.		
described all of the important details in each photo.		
pointed out important similarities and differences between the two photos.		
explained clearly how modern communication devices can bring younger and older people together (Partner B) / can help older people (Partner A).		
spoke for about three minutes.		

c **Listen to Partner A. S/He should speak for about three minutes.**

d **Take Partner A's book. Fill in the feedback form for him/her.**

e **Talk together about your photos for about five minutes. Compare and contrast the situations.**
In addition to the points mentioned in the feedback form, you need to listen to your partner in a dialogue. React to your partner's statements: agree, disagree and add aspects. SF 12 → SB p. 135

Guided writing

In your final English exams, you have a choice of two guided writing tasks. Genres (text types) include letters and emails (often to apply for a job), stories, blog entries and newspaper articles. The **genre** required is highlighted in the task.

1 Choosing a task

a Read the tasks.

TASK A	Walker's Electronics
Write a **letter of application** for the job offered on the right. **Include the following aspects:** • reasons for applying • personal qualifications • job details • ideas about what types of products to sell and why Find a suitable beginning and ending. **Write about 180 words.** You need not write any addresses.	Part-time shop assistant for family firm required. You are an independent, organized young person with a good knowledge of digital and electronic devices.

TASK B	*Digital detox*
Continue the story. Include the following aspects: • reasons for a digital detox • positive aspects • negative aspects • a happy ending **Write about 180 words.** Do not copy the beginning of the story.	*After I got my first smartphone, I began to use social media a lot. I had lots of friends and followers and I got many likes. But then I decided to do a digital detox for a month ...*

b **Choose the task that is easier for you to complete.**
Did your class just practise writing letters of application? Do you love writing stories? Do you know a lot of vocabulary connected with one of the task topics? Choose that task.

2 Preparing to write

a **Analyze the task.**
Are you writing as yourself or another person? Who are you writing for (audience)? What is the aim of the text? What should it include (content points)? What vocabulary do you need?

b **Find three details for each of the content points (the aspects your text should include).**
You can invent details. When writing your text, don't just list them, describe and explain.

Aspect / Content point	Detail 1	Detail 2	Detail 3
1			
2			
3			
4			

3 Writing and checking your text

a **Write the letter of application or continue the story you have prepared.** SF 5+22 → SB pp. 130 + 144–145
Connect your sentences and ideas with each other (linking words). Give your text a sensible structure. A letter of application, for example, requires formal language and a standard structure.

Save time counting words: Count the words in three lines and then find out your average number (Ø) of words per line.

b **Check (✓) your text.**
Are all words spelled correctly? Did you use synonyms to avoid repetition? Is your grammar correct? Did you use linking words? Are all content points included and fully elaborated?

Indian images

Unit 4

Words and pictures

1 LISTENING A German-Indian exchange programme

16 **a** Marie's school in Germany has organized an exchange programme with a school in Pune, India. Listen to Marie talk about her group's experiences. Write down the main things she talks about. You don't have to write complete sentences, but one word is not enough.

Day 1	
Day 2	
Day 3	
Day 4	
Day 5	
Day 6	

b Talk to your partner and compare your lists.

c Look at the pictures. Use your notes from a to match the pictures (A–F) with the number of the day (1–6) on which she saw and did these things.

A

3

C

2

E

6

B

5

D

4

F

1

SB pp. 58–59

Four profiles

1 Working in India

a Find nouns from the texts on SB pp. 60–61 to complete the networks.

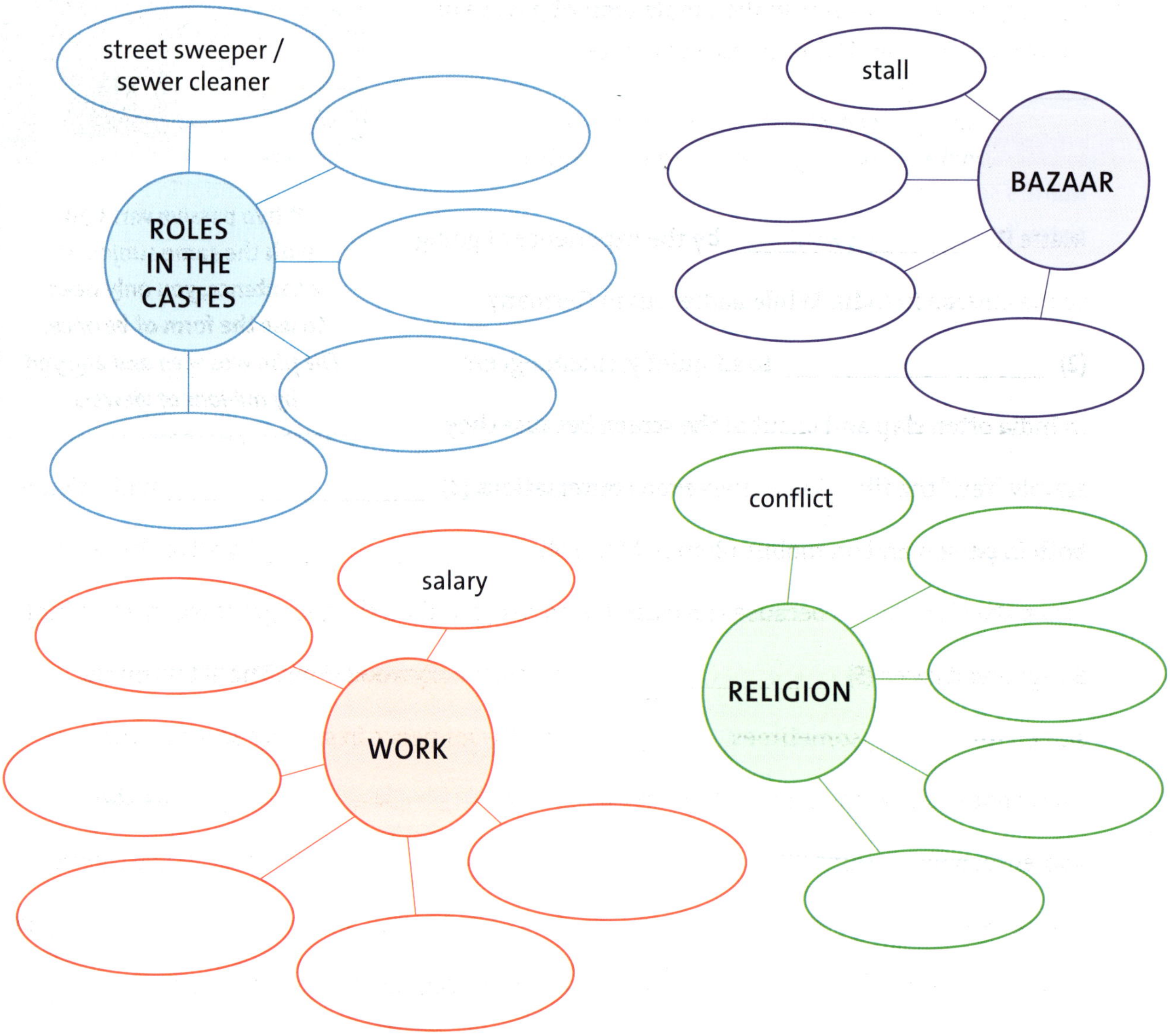

b Look at the four profiles on SB pp. 60–61. Find a word or expression which means the same as each of the words below. There is one example (0) at the beginning.

0 wages (profile A)	*salary*
1 rubbish (profile A)	
2 (to) keep away from (profile A)	
3 problem (profile B)	
4 nearly (profile C)	
5 (to) move up (profile C)	
6 largest group (profile D)	

SB pp. 60–61

Indian cinema

1 REVISION Going to the cinema in India

Complete the text about Marie's visit to an Indian cinema by using the correct verbs in the simple present passive or simple past passive. Use each verb only once.

annoy • expect • hold • include • join • make • show • speak • ~~surprise~~ • watch

If two passive verbs go with the same subject in a sentence, you only need to use the form of *be* once: *The film was <u>seen</u> and <u>enjoyed</u> by millions of viewers.*

Marie (1) *was* *surprised* by the experience of going to the cinema in India. While audiences in Germany (2) ________ ____________ to sit quietly, cinema-goers in India often clap and shout at the screen because they simply "feel" the film. Sometimes even conversations (3) ________ ____________ with friends both in person and on mobile phones. Marie (4) ________ ____________ by all of the noise when the film started because she wasn't used to it, but then she thought it was a lot of fun! Songs and dances (5) ________ ____________ in most Bollywood films. The actors on the screen (6) ________ sometimes ____________ by the audience in singing and dancing. Marie noticed that some of the lines in the film (7) ________ also ____________ by the audience: popular films (8) ________ sometimes ____________ several times in the cinema. One of India's most popular films, Dilwale Dulhania Le Jayenge, (9) ________ ____________ in 1995 and (10) ____________ every day in a cinema in Mumbai for over 20 years.

SB p. 62

17 2 LISTENING Dilwale Dulhania Le Jayenge

Listen to Chirag telling Marie about DDLJ. Then complete the sentences with passive verb forms.

1 DDLJ will be ____________________ tonight at a cinema near Chirag's house.

2 The title can be ____________________ as *The Brave-Hearted Will Take the Bride.*

3 Chiraq says that it ____________________ seen by anyone interested in Bollywood films.

4 The film ____________________ translated into English.

5 It ____________________ shown with English subtitles tonight.

6 Tickets can be ____________________ on the cinema's website.

7 A documentary about the making of the film ____________________ watched online.

8 A documentary like that ____________________ made before in India.

SB p. 63

3 Mobile cinemas

Complete the text. Fill in the correct passive form.

Although Bollywood is such a huge industry, relatively few cinemas (1) *are built* (build) in India. Films (2) __________ (show) on only about 9,000 big screens there, compared with about 40,000 in the US and China. Most cinemas are in cities: films often (3) __________ (can/not/watch) in a cinema by people living in small villages in the country. This situation (4) __________ (recently/improve) by businesspeople such as Sushil Chaudhary, whose company PictureTime (5) __________ (found) in 2015. More than 40 mobile cinemas (6) __________ (already/build) by PictureTime. They (7) __________ (transport) around the country by trucks and (8) __________ (blow up) like balloons. They (9) __________ (can/set up) in about two hours. The air in the cinemas (10) __________ (cool) for the customers. It was hard to start the business. After the company (11) __________ (prevent) from showing some popular films, they (12) __________ (finally/give) permission by a few film companies to show big Bollywood films. What plans (13) __________ (make) for the next few years? The number of trucks (14) __________ (will/increase) to several thousand: they (15) __________ (will/send) all over the country to bring big screens to small places. SB pp. 62–63

4 Luxury cinemas

Some Indian luxury cinemas offer special services: for example, you can have your glasses cleaned. Make sentences, using *have* and the main verb.

1 You / can / a film of your choice / show.

____.

2 You / can / food / bring / to your seats.

____.

3 You / can / your car / park / at the cinema.

____.

4 You / can / feet / massage / before the film.

____. SB p. 63

Taking part in a discussion

1 Delhi's odd-even rule

a Read the information about Delhi's odd-even rule.

In 2016, Delhi introduced a so-called odd-even rule to reduce air pollution from cars. In certain months on even days (for example, the 2nd, 4th, etc. of a month) only cars with number plates ending in an even number can be driven and only odd-numbered cars on odd days (e.g. the 3rd, 5th, etc.). The rule has been repeated several times.

b Brainstorm the advantages and disadvantages of this rule with a partner. Make notes.

Advantages	Disadvantages

18 c Listen to a conversation about the rule. Then add new arguments to your list in b. SB p. 64

2 Discussion phrases

a Write one or more appropriate phrase(s) to use in each situation.

The situation	You say ...
1 You're giving your opinion.	*In my opinion, /*
2 Someone has spoken while you were speaking.	
3 You want to speak while someone else is speaking.	
4 You express a different opinion.	
5 You like the idea that has just been mentioned.	
6 You briefly mention other information.	
7 You do/think the same thing as someone else.	

b Discuss the odd-even rule with a partner, giving your opinion on whether it would be a good idea for the city you live in or one near you and why (not). Use phrases from a and SB p. 64. SB p. 64

An email with personal opinions

1 Fact or opinion?

a **Read the email. Find and highlight nine sentences that give Leela's personal opinions.**

Hi there!
Great to hear from you! One and two-child laws in India are a great topic for your presentation. These laws already exist in some areas. However, there are arguments for the laws as well as against them.
I can start you off with some background information and my opinion on the issue. India's population is huge and a lot of Indians are poor. So, some politicians have suggested and passed laws saying that people can only have one or two children. These laws aren't a good idea. As in many other countries, one main problem is a lack of health education. Couples should have access to health services and contraceptives*, and not be forced by the government to have fewer children.
Many researchers have found that children without brothers and sisters are very lonely. In addition, later in life they often have to take care of their old parents by themselves. That is why being an only child can be sad and hard.
Surveys show that many people in India still think that it's better to have sons than daughters.
If families can only have one or two children, then a lot of families will only want to have boys.
One-child laws in China meant that some families killed baby girls. This shouldn't happen in India!
What is more, experts on the economy say that if families have fewer children, we won't have enough workers to keep our country's economy healthy and growing. They predict that there will be lots of old people and not enough young people to pay for their care.
So what's best for India? It's important to pass new laws about sustainable development, reducing pollution and resource planning. However, a one-child law isn't an effective strategy.
Anyhow, I hope this helps and I'd be interested in your thoughts on this topic and how your presentation went.
Yours
Leela

*contraceptives Verhütungsmittel

b **Add phrases from the box to five sentences you highlighted in a so that they can clearly be recognized as opinions and not facts. You won't need all the phrases. There are several possible solutions.**

In my opinion, ... • I believe that ... • I think it's true that ... • ~~I think ...~~ • In my view, ... • I agree that India's population is huge, but ... • My view is that ...

1 *I think,* ______
2 ______
3 ______
4 ______
5 ______

SB p. 65

2 Your answer to Leela

Write a reply to Leela. Thank her for her help and tell her how your presentation went. Then give your opinion about these laws. Include phrases from 1 b and SB pp. 64–65 that show which statements are your opinion. Find a suitable beginning and ending for your email. Write about 180 words.

SB p. 65

Lion

1 READING Saroo's story

a Read the story on SB pp. 66–67 and sentences 1–8. What is true, false or not in the text? Tick (✓) the correct boxes.

	true	false	not in the text
1 Saroo's father died when he was a baby.	☐	☐	☐
2 Saroo always spent a lot of time with his brothers.	☐	☐	☐
3 Saroo sometimes used to travel by train with his brothers.	☐	☐	☐
4 His brothers had good jobs at the train station in Berampur.	☐	☐	☐
5 Saroo felt happy when he was with his brothers.	☐	☐	☐
6 Guddu owned a bike.	☐	☐	☐
7 Guddu played a trick on Saroo by hiding from him.	☐	☐	☐
8 Saroo woke up on the train and ran from carriage to carriage.	☐	☐	☐

b Explain why you picked 'true', 'false' or 'not in the text' for each answer in a.

1 *The story doesn't mention Saroo's father.*

2 ______

3 ______

4 ______

5 ______

6 ______

7 ______

8 ______ SB pp. 66–68

2 Kolkata's railway children

Complete the text. Write one word for each gap.

Even today, according (1) ______ one charity, over 250,000 children live on the streets of Kolkata. Over one thousand children (2) ______ found every year at Sealdah, one of the city's largest railway (3) ______. Some have run away, some have (4) ______ sent away by poor families and (5) ______ are just looking for work. Many children live (6) ______ the station, either (7) ______ or with their families. There are several charities that try to help the children, by (8) ______ their families or by placing (9) ______ in a new home. SB pp. 66–68

3 Words that go together

a Read definitions 1–5 and fill in the missing word in each collocation. You can find the collocations in the information box and text on SB pp. 66–67.

Collocations are usual combinations of words in a language.
For example, the English way of saying 'ein Baby bekommen' is *to have a baby*, not *to ~~get~~ a baby*.

1 *a place where construction takes place:* building ____________
2 *to use your time:* to ____________ time
3 *to become friends with someone:* to ____________ a friend
4 *the place where a town ends:* the ____________ of town
5 *to start sleeping:* to ____________ asleep

A phrasal verb is made of a verb and a preposition or an adverb. You usually can't figure out its meaning by using logic: you need to learn each phrasal verb. For example: *to drop out (of school)* = '(die Schule) abbrechen', *to go off* = 'klingeln/losgehen'

b Circle the right word to complete each phrasal verb from the story.

1 Saroo's mother wasn't always able to look *for / after / on* the children.
2 She didn't earn enough money for the family to live *on / with / of*.
3 Saroo used to like hanging *by / to / around* with his older brothers.
4 Saroo and Guddu got *off / out / from* the train in Berampur.
5 Saroo waited *on / to / for* his brother alone on the platform.

SB pp. 66-68

4 Advice for Saroo

a What advice would you give five-year-old Saroo? Write down four ideas. The words in the box may help you. Use the imperative or modal verbs.

always • don't • make sure • never • stay

Always tell your mother where you're going. · You should never get on a train alone. · ...

1 ____________________
2 ____________________
3 ____________________
4 ____________________

b Discuss your ideas with a partner. Use phrases from SB p. 64 to agree or disagree. SB pp. 66-68

5 Helping homeless children in India

a Today there are many organizations that help homeless children in India. Do online research on one of these organizations. Try to answer the following questions.

- What is the organization called and when was it founded?
- What kind of group runs the organization (private, religious, government, etc.)?
- How does the organization help children?
- How many children has it helped?

b Make a leaflet and present your organization to your class. SB pp. 66-68

The Golden Triangle

1 MEDIATION Travel tips

Verwende die Informationen aus folgendem Text. Bearbeite die Aufgaben (1–6) stichpunktartig auf Deutsch. Es ist keine wörtliche Übersetzung nötig, die Aspekte müssen inhaltlich jedoch vollständig erfasst sein. Einzelwörter genügen nicht als Antwort.

Tips for independent travellers to the Golden Triangle

The busiest tourist season is from October until March. If you go outside of this period, there will be fewer tourists but it is likely to be incredibly hot.

We recommend travelling around the Golden Triangle by express train. You will have a more authentic experience than on a tourist coach. You don't need to worry about big crowds or the stereotypical images of people riding on top of trains and hanging out of the windows. On an express train you'll have a safe and comfortable trip from one city to another. You must buy tickets online or at a railway station before you get on the train. At the station, find a porter in a red jacket and wearing a badge to help you get to your train and carry your bags: this is a great service and will cost you around 80 rupees (about € 1).

In the cities, parks are a place to find quiet beauty without lots of people. Go to the big attractions early in the morning or in the late afternoon to avoid crowds. You will also enjoy cooler temperatures. Bonus: the sight of the Taj Mahal in the light of a sunrise is beautiful.

To get around within cities, take an autorickshaw (also called a three-wheeler): they're the best way to get through the traffic. Find out the price from the driver before you get in.

Many tourists suffer from *Delhi belly*, which means stomach

problems from unsafe water. How can you protect yourself? You can use tablets to clean the water, but some people don't like the taste. You can easily buy bottled water, but check that the bottle has not already been opened. Eat only food that is hot and freshly cooked. Don't eat fruit and vegetables that haven't been cooked because they might have been washed in unclean water.

1 Was sind ein Vor- und ein Nachteil von Reisen außerhalb der Hauptsaison? ______

______

2 Was sind die Vorteile einer Fahrt mit einem Expresszug? (3 Details) ______

______

3 Welche Ratschläge für eine Zugreise werden gegeben? (2 Details) ______

______

4 Wie kann man größere Menschenmengen in Städten vermeiden? (2 Details) ______

______

5 Welches Transportmittel für innerstädtische Reisen wird empfohlen and warum? ______

______

6 Wie kann man eine häufige Reisekrankheit vermeiden? (3 Details) ______

______

______

SB p. 70

Evaluating sources

1 Evaluation checklist

a You are preparing a presentation on outsourcing to India and find the two texts below. Read each text, then use the checklist to evaluate each source. Tick (✓) Yes, No or ? if you are not sure or it is not relevant for this source. Green boxes mean that this may be a good source; red boxes mean that you should be careful.

	Text 1			Text 2		
	Yes	No	?	Yes	No	?
Is the text from a source you know or which seems reliable?	☐	☐	☐	☐	☐	☐
Is the author named? Is the name linked to a biography?	☐	☐	☐	☐	☐	☐
Are there mistakes in language, design, etc.?	☐	☐	☐	☐	☐	☐
Does it contain information that seems hard to believe?	☐	☐	☐	☐	☐	☐
Does it make promises or try to trick you?	☐	☐	☐	☐	☐	☐
Is it trying to sell something?	☐	☐	☐	☐	☐	☐
Is the information in the text fact?	☐	☐	☐	☐	☐	☐
If it is an opinion, is it clearly identified as one?	☐	☐	☐	☐	☐	☐
Does the text quote or link to official/expert sources?	☐	☐	☐	☐	☐	☐
Was it a paid search engine result?	☐	☐	☐	☐	☐	☐

www.example.com/highqualityoutsourcingindia

Outsourcing to India

India is the international leader in providing highly skilled and talented workers for IT and other industries. Over three million graduates join the workforce every year. India is also the world's largest English-speaking country, adding to its appeal to businesses. One American manager says, "The quality our product has increased 100 % since we began outsourcing work to a company in Hyderabad."

High quality, low cost

The low cost of living in India means that workers typically earn much less than in developed countries. A highly skilled software developer in the U.S. can earn up to $80 an hour, while one with the same qualifications in India may only earn $15 an hour. This can translate into big savings for YOUR company. Contact us for more information.

THE NEW YORK NEWS

Outsourcing Faces Increasing Criticism

By HEERA SAVADI

Outsourcing to India has become a common, if not always popular, practice of American companies, primarily in software development and call centers. Jobs are not done by workers within the company itself, but sent to outside companies, either within the U.S. or in other countries.

The practice is controversial. Companies which outsource jobs say that it saves money, making their products and services less expensive for customers and clients. They also say that it's not always possible to find qualified workers in the U.S., particularly when their business has grown quickly or has new needs.

Those against outsourcing say that jobs should be given to American workers, not foreigners. Others claim that the quality of outsourced work is not always high.

b Discuss your results from a with a partner.

c Find and print out two more texts on outsourcing from the internet. Present them to your class and say whether you think they are reliable sources or not and why. Use the checklist for help.

SB p. 71

1 Check your vocabulary

You can find the answers to these tasks on pages 65-66.

Complete the sentences with the correct words. The mixed letters at the end can help you.

1 There is a huge __________ between the lives of the very rich and the very poor. **carttons**

2 The __________ rate in India is lower among women than among men. **articley**

3 Discrimination against lower __________ is illegal in India, but still happens. **cestas**

4 More people from lower castes have been put into government jobs by __________. **sqatou**

5 I have a lot of things __________ because I don't have time to go shopping. **revdiedel**

6 Putting rubbish and waste in rivers __________ the water. **outspell**

7 I wish you wouldn't __________ me all the time. **pruntiret**

8 He reads his __________ every day, although he doesn't really believe in it. **choopoers**

9 We were __________ to see our photos in the newspaper. **delhiltr**

10 They took an autorickshaw around Agra, looking at the __________. **chaircuttere**

2 Check your language

a **Complete the text about an Indian film by filling in the correct passive form of each verb.**

This film **(1)** __________ (make) about 10 years ago. It **(2)** __________ (include) in a lot of "Best films of all time" lists. The star **(3)** __________ (not offer) a role in it, but he asked the director to let him try out for the lead role.

The film **(4)** __________ (set) in a small Indian village in the 19th century.

It **(5)** __________ (show) on TV later tonight and I think it **(6)** __________ (watch) by a lot of people. Our teacher said it **(7)** __________ (see) by anyone who doesn't already know it.

b **Write suitable questions and answers in the passive.**

1 Can seats be reserved?
Yes, __________.

2 Will the platform number be shown on the board?
Yes, __________.

3 Is food served on the train?
Yes, __________.

4 __________ online?
No, the tickets were booked here at the train station.

5 __________?
Yes, the tickets were paid for when they were booked.

3 Check your writing

Complete the words and phrases to express opinions in the email.

Dear Mathilda

In your email you mentioned that you would be interested in riding an elephant in India, so I wanted to give you m_____ o_________ of this activity.

There is a lot of discussion about elephant riding. Some tourists have seen images of people riding elephants and have this experience on their must-do lists for India. I_____ m_____ v________, riding an elephant isn't a good idea. They are s______ t_____ b_____ taken from their mothers as babies and you can see that they are often treated badly. Some places offering elephant rides now call themselves rescue centres, but I d______ b________ that the elephants are treated any better there than in other places. B_____ t_____ way, some animal rights groups are trying to get elephant rides banned (like circuses with animals in Germany and the US), so you might not be allowed to ride one anyhow.

While it's necessary to support India's tourism industry, i_____ also i__________ to protect animals! I a________ that riding elephants could be a fun experience, but I s________ b________ that it's wrong to do it.

Yours

Nagesh

4 Check your mediation skills

Verwende die Informationen aus dem Text und bearbeite die Aufgaben (1–6) stichpunktartig auf Deutsch. Einzelwörter genügen nicht als Antwort.

AMBER FORT TOUR

Discover incredible Amber Fort, a group of beautiful temples, gardens and palaces.

Your day

You will be picked up at your hotel in Jaipur by a private car and taken to the fort. Your professional personal guide will walk with you to the top of the hill to see the amazing architecture and fabulous views. You'll see Hawa Mahal, the Palace of Winds, and hear about Amber Fort's history from your guide, who will be happy to answer your questions.

Booking

Reserve your places online or by phone at least two days before your visit. You will receive an email with your ticket: print it out or just show it on your smartphone. You may cancel your ticket up to three days before the tour.

1 Was ist die Festung Amber?
2 Wie kommt man dorthin, wenn man diese Führung bucht?
3 Was beinhaltet die Führung?
4 Wie bucht man die Führung?
5 Muss man die Karten ausdrucken?
6 Unter welchen Bedingungen kann man die Buchung wieder stornieren?

Unit 1

SKILLS TRAINING Speaking course 1 exercise 2c | page 9

2 SPEAKING **At a hostel**

c **Partner A**

You're a German teenager visiting Sydney for the first time. You meet an American teenager in your hostel.

- Ask where he or she has already been in Sydney.
- Ask which activity he or she would most recommend and why.
- Say if you think that sounds good and why.
- Say thank you and goodbye.

You start.

Partner B

You're an American teenager visiting Sydney. You meet a German teenager in your hostel.

- Tell him/her that you've been to Harbour Bridge, Luna Park and on a boat ride around the harbour.
- Recommend climbing Harbour Bridge with a guided group: fun, challenging, a little scary, great view.
- Say goodbye.

Your partner starts.

SB p. 15

STUDY SKILLS exercise 1 | page 11

1 SPEAKING AND LISTENING **Sports collocations**

a **Complete the questions with *do, go* or *play*. Use a dictionary if you need help.**

1 Would you like to ____________ snorkelling or scuba-diving?

2 How do you ____________ badminton?

3 Do you like to watch other people ____________ team sports?

4 Do you sometimes ____________ sports in a gym? Why or why not?

5 Do you think that it's fun to ____________ fishing? Why or why not?

19 b **Listen and check.**

c **Ask your partner the questions from a as well as two more questions about sports. In your questions you should use *do, go* or *play*. Write down his or her answers. Report to the class.**

d **When do you use *do, go* and *play*? Write rules for each word.**

SB p. 20

Skills practice

exercise 3 | page 15

3 SPEAKING A phone call

a You work in the office of an exchange programme. A student is calling for information about a trip to Australia next week. Answer and ask questions with the help of the prompts below. You start. Take notes.

Name of student: ______________________

Email address: ______________________

Phone number: ______________________

1	Answer the phone. You are Kim Meyer from International Language Experience. Ask how you can help the caller.
3	Ask the caller politely to spell his/her name.
5	Say thank you and tell the caller which flight s/he is going to take (WXY2993).
7	Tell the caller when the flight leaves (9.35 am) and arrives (the next day at 3 pm).
9	Ask the caller for his/her email address and say why you need it (to send the ticket).
11	Spell your first name and last name (Kim Meyer). Ask the caller politely for his/her phone number and say why you need it (to inform him/her about any changes or to give further important information).

b Your partner should check your notes.

exercise 2 | page 16

2 REVISION Talking about charts and diagrams

a Use charts A and B to complete the questions below.

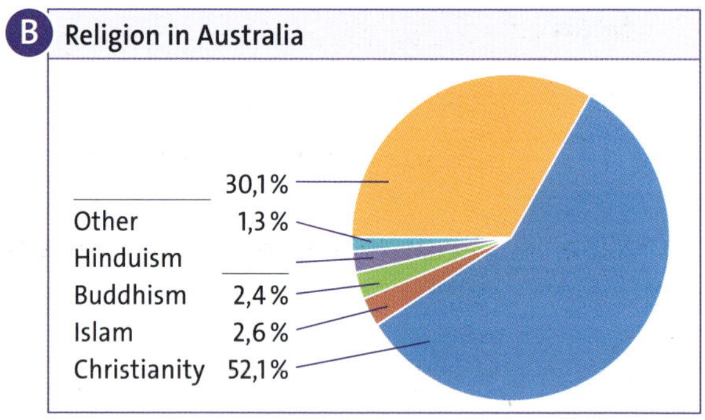

Source charts A and B: Based on ABS, Census of Population and Housing 2016

1 (A) How many Australian citizens were born ______________?

2 (A) ______________ were 167,000 Australian citizens born?

3 (B) What do a little less than *(fraction)* ______________ of Australians give as their religion?

4 (B) What ______________ of Australians are Hindu?

b Ask your partner for the missing information in the charts. Write the answers in the charts.

c Describe chart B to partner B.

• What kind of chart is it? • What does it show? • What is the most interesting information in the chart (e.g. highs and lows)?

Unit 2

WORDS AND PICTURES exercise 1 | page 17

1 SPEAKING Part-time jobs

a Hazel and Shevon are talking about their part-time jobs. Put Shevon's lines in the right places. There are three extra lines.

Hazel: Do you have a part-time job?

Shevon: ____________________

But there's always time to read a little.

Hazel: Oh, that's cool! How many hours a week do you work?

Shevon: ____________________

__________ and four hours on Saturdays.

Do you work?

Hazel: Yes, I have a job with a gardening company.

Shevon: ____________________

Hazel: A lot of hard, dirty work! I dig holes, put the plants in, carry heavy bags ... but I like it!

Shevon: ____________________

Hazel: Twelve dollars. What does the library pay?

Shevon: ____________________

Hazel: Are you saving for college?

Shevon: ____________________

Hazel: I'll need to pay my living expenses, but my parents will pay the fees.

Do you like your job? • Do you work every day? • How much do you get an hour? • I work three hours a day after school twice a week • No, I don't work. • No, my parents say they'll pay for it. • Not that much: only eleven dollars. • What do you do? • Yes, I work at the library, shelving books.

08 b Listen to the dialogue and check your answers.

c Read the dialogue with your partner.

SB p. 25

INTRODUCTION exercise 4 | page 20

4 REVISION A presentation about Girl Scouts

You are preparing a presentation on Girl Scouts in Germany with your partner. Ask and answer questions about what you have learned so far with the help of the prompts below.
Your partner starts.

2 They • be founded • in Georgia • in 1912.

3 How long • Girl Scouts • be • in Germany?

6 They • earn badges • by • volunteer • and • go camping.

7 Where • they • go camping • this year?

SB pp. 28-29

Unit 2

SKILLS TRAINING Speaking course 2 exercise 3 | page 23

3 SPEAKING Making formal phone calls

a You are a British parent whose family has just moved to Germany for your new job with an international company. As the family doesn't speak German yet, you are looking for a babysitter who can speak English. Fill in the information about your requirements below.

b Then talk to the caller. Make sure to arrange a time for an interview.

Number of children	
Days babysitter needed	
Number of hours a day	
Address	
Near public transport?	
Pay (per hour)	

Interview scheduled for ______________________________

c After the conversation, compare your notes with your partner's notes. SB p. 32

SKILLS TRAINING Mediation exercise 1 | page 26

1 SPEAKING Working conditions

Describe the five words in the box to your partner. Your partner needs to guess the word described. Take turns.

self-employed • full-time • boss • abroad • internship

You use this word to say that someone has time and is free to do something.

Available?

SB p. 36

Unit 2

SKILLS TRAINING Speaking course 2 exercise 3 | page 23

3 SPEAKING **Making formal phone calls**

a You are a German teenager who is calling about this advert for a position as a babysitter. Use the keywords below to write down questions about the job.

Babysitter needed
British family looking for a high school student to babysit twice a week. Must speak English and enjoy working with children.
Please call 0162 2082784 after 5 pm.

b Then talk to the parent and write down her/his answers.

Keywords	Question	Answer
Number of children?	*How many children do you have?*	
Days babysitter needed?		
Number of hours a day?		
Address?		
Near public transport?		
Pay (per hour)?		

Interview scheduled for ______________________________

c After the conversation, compare your notes with your partner's notes. SB p. 32

SKILLS TRAINING Mediation exercise 1 | page 26

1 SPEAKING **Working conditions**

Describe the five words in the box to your partner. Your partner needs to guess the word described. Take turns.

automation • apprenticeship • satisfactory • flexible • part-time

SB p. 36

Exam practice

exercise 1 | page 41

1 SPEAKING Older people and modern communication devices

a **Listen to Partner B. S/He should speak for about three minutes.**

b **Take Partner B's book and fill in the feedback form for him/her.**

c **Talk to Partner B.**

1 Describe each photo. Look at SF 10 SB p. 133 for help.
Describe the people and places, objects, positions and activities.

2 Compare and contrast the situations shown in the photos.
Compare: How are the people/objects/situations similar?
Contrast: How are they different?

3 How can modern communication devices help older people?
Use the photos to develop your ideas. How are communication devices helping older people here? Can you think of other ways?

In the photo on the left there's a ... A person is ...

Both photos show ... In the photo on the right we can see ..., but in the photo on the left ...

Communication devices can help older people to ... Older people can also use devices to ...

d **Give your book to Partner B, so s/he can fill in the feedback form on page 41.**

e **Talk together about your photos for about five minutes. Compare and contrast the situations.**
In addition to the points mentioned in the feedback form, you need to listen to your partner in a dialogue. React to your partner's statements: agree, disagree and add aspects. SF 12 → SB p. 135

Unit 1 p. 13, p. 14

1 Check your vocabulary

a An Iranian writer who spent six years in an Australian **(1)** *detention centre / prison / community* on an island in Papua New Guinea has arrived in New Zealand. Behrouz Boochani was allowed to leave to accept a prize he won for a book he wrote by text messages. He says he will never **(2)** *bear / return / deny* to the country.

Boochani's book describes how he arrived on the island and his life there. He says that writing helped him to live through the **(3)** *authority / indignity / testimony* that the centre **(4)** *ignored / integrated / inflicted* on him.

Boochani left his home country for political reasons. He travelled to Indonesia, where he got on a boat to Australia with other refugees. The first boat broke and he nearly **(5)** *separated / drowned / drank*. The second boat arrived in Australian waters but was stopped: he and his **(6)** *fellow / regular / direct* passengers were sent to an Australian detention centre in Papua New Guinea.

b
1. The Australian prime minister apologized *to* the stolen generations in 2008.
2. Thousands of Aboriginal families were broken *up* between 1910 and the 1970s.
3. Indigenous children suffered *from* being separated from their parents.
4. They were brought *up* in children's homes, where they were forced to soak *up* everything they were taught about a strange culture.
5. Parents weren't allowed to pass *on* their culture to their children.
6. Children were told to cut *out* the talk about their families.
7. Families used to dream *about/of* finding each other again.

2 Check your language

Hello from the famous Bondi Beach! *We are surfing* here today! Soft sand, warm water, huge waves: *it feels* like paradise! *I had booked* a surfing lesson before *we came* to Australia. I didn't want to miss the chance to experience this!

While *I was getting ready* this morning, *I found* a huge spider in my bag! *I used to be* scared of all spiders, but now I'm just scared of the Australian ones!

3 Check your mediation skills

Brother: Wie heißt diese Schnecke? Und ist sie giftig?

You: *Excuse me, please. Can you tell me what this snail is called? And is it venomous?*

Lifeguard: Oh, that's a cone snail. Good that it's empty. They are dangerous if they are still alive! The ones you find in the water are very venomous. Don't pick them up ... or step on them!

You: *Das ist eine Kegelschnecke. Die lebendigen im Wasser sind gefährlich und sehr giftig. Man darf sie nicht in die Hand nehmen oder drauftreten.*
Brother: Was passiert, wenn man gestochen wird?
You: *What happens if they sting you / if you get stung?*
Lifeguard: You have to go to hospital. There's no antivenom, but the doctors can help.
You: *Man muss ins Krankenhaus. Es gibt zwar kein Gegengift, aber die Ärzte können einem helfen.*

4 Check your speaking skills

a **Teacher:** Welcome to our class. Can you tell us a little about yourself?
You: *(My name is Moritz Meyer and I'm from a small village in Bavaria, Germany.)*
Student 1: Why did you want to spend a year in Australia?
You: *(I wanted to experience life in an English-speaking country. I think Australia is very cool: amazing animals, beautiful beaches, fascinating culture.)*
Student 2: How did you learn to speak English?
You: *(We learn it at school and I also read and watch a lot of movies in English.)*
You: *(Have you been to Germany or do you speak German?)*
Student 1: I've never been to Germany, but I'm learning German now.
You: *(What sports do you play here?)*
Student 2: This week we are playing soccer, but next week we'll start doing yoga.
You: *(Where can I sit / Is there a free seat anywhere?)*
Teacher: You can sit at that empty desk near the window.
You: *(Thank you / Thanks.)*

Unit 2 p. 27, p. 28

1 Check your vocabulary

a Someone who …

1 comes and does things on time is … — *j* punctual
2 tells the truth and doesn't steal is … — *c* honest
3 does things with and for people to make it easier for them is … — *b* helpful
4 acts in a way that is open and kind is … — *i* friendly
5 waits without being annoyed is … — *e* patient
6 is able to produce something new, especially art, is … — *k* creative
7 is good at planning and keeping things tidy and available is … — *d* organized
8 does what he/she is supposed to do is … — *h* responsible
9 behaves politely to people, especially people like parents, teachers and bosses, is … — *g* respectful

b *2* **a** Write a cover letter
4 **b** Arrange an interview
3 **c** Send your application
5 **d** Attend the interview
1 **e** Read a job advertisement
6 **f** Write a thank-you note to the interviewer

2 Check your language

Q: Why have you applied for this job?

A: I **(1)** *saw* the advert and **(2)** *thought* I would be perfect for the position.

Q: Had you already heard of our company?

A: Yes, I **(3)** *'ve/have used* your products for years.

Q: Have you ever had a difficult boss?

A: No, I **(4)** *'ve/have been* lucky: they **(5)** *were / have been* very easy to work for!

Q: What are you going to do after you leave school?

A: I **(6)** *'m/am going to travel* around the US this summer. In autumn I **(7)** *'ll/will probably start* an apprenticeship.

Q: Where do you think you'll be in five years?

A: I hope I **(8)** *'ll/will have* a job in a bank.

3 Check your speaking

a **Man:** Hello?

You: *(Hello. My name is ... I'm calling about the advert for a dog walker.)*

Introduce yourself and say why you are calling.

Man: Oh, wonderful. Do you have experience of dog walking?

You: *(Yes. I walk my family's three dogs every day and I also walk our neighbours' dogs when they're on holiday.)*

Say yes and tell him a little about it.

Man: That sounds perfect. C&#?d !$u *$m/ f&r an §?#erv*%w on Tuesday &# &#?! &#?

You: *(I'm sorry, I didn't catch that. The line is very bad.)*

Tell him politely that you couldn't hear that.

Man: Could you come for an interview on Tuesday at 6 pm?

You: *(I'm sorry, I don't have time on Tuesday. I have football practice on Tuesday evenings.)*

Tell him that you don't have time on Tuesday and why.

Man: What about Wednesday at 4 pm?

You: *(Yes, I'm available then. Thank you.)*

Agree to this time. Thank him.

Man: You're welcome. I'll see you then.

You: *(I'm looking forward to meeting you. Goodbye.)*

End the call politely.

4 Check your writing

Education	2019 – present Figgleston Secondary School
Training	2019 Completed volunteer art teacher training, Figgleston library
Work experience	2021 – present Volunteer art teacher, Figgleston library
Personal statement	As a very creative person, I'm looking for a position ...
Digital skills	Microsoft Word, Microsoft PowerPoint, photo editing
Organizational skills	Planning activities for large groups ...
Communication skills	Presenting, demonstrating and explaining activities ...
Languages	First languages: English and French; Foreign language: Spanish

Unit 3 p. 39, p. 40

1 Check your vocabulary

a
1 Eric is always careful about *logging off* his computer when he's finished using it.
2 We prefer *streaming* movies and shows to watching them on TV.
3 She *scrolled* down to read the comments after she finished the article.
4 Somebody guessed my *password* and *hacked* into my account.
5 Turn off all of your *electronic* devices until the plane has landed.
6 Try *resetting* your device if it's not working correctly.
7 You can do that by *pressing* the button on the side of the device.
8 She updates her *status* every couple of hours, but I hardly ever do that.

b

1 *50 % cheaper*	50 % off
2 During one of these, a store sells things for less money than the usual price.	*sale*
3 *a promise by a company to repair or replace a broken item*	warranty
4 *to use*	to consume
5 A large shop is made up of several of these, each selling a different kind of things.	*department*

2 Check your language

b
You: Andy called me last night. He was talking about **(1)** *his party there today*.
Artea: Did he say when we should be there?
You: He said **(2)** *we could come at 7 pm*. He **(3)** *told me/us to be* on time. And he asked me **(4)** *how long we could stay*.
Artea: My mum said she'd pick us up at 11 pm. Did he say anything about food and drinks?
You: Yes. He said **(5)** *that he had bought* a lot of food **(6)** *yesterday* and that Sterling **(7)** *was bringing drinks*.
Artea: Did he tell you how many people are coming?
You: He said **(8)** *that he was only allowed to invite* ten friends. And he asked me **(9)** *not to tell anyone about* the party.

3 Check your mediation skills

You: Hast du die App schon installiert? Und ist die Birne schon in der Lampe?
Oma: Ja.
You: Prima. Nun Schritt 2: *Schalte das Gerät / die Lampe ein.*
Und Schritt 3: *Öffne die App. Klicke auf das Haus-Symbol unten auf dem Bildschirm.*
Oma: Mache ich. Und nun?
You: *Klicke auf das Plus-Symbol oben auf dem Bildschirm.* Und dann im Menü links auf das Wort „Light".
Oma: OK.
You: Ich hatte für dich ja bereits ein Smart&Bright-Konto eingerichtet. *Logge dich da bitte ein.*

Oma: Moment ... Ja, es hat geklappt.
You: Super. *Ist deine neue Birne* auf dem Bildschirm erschienen?
Oma: Ja!
You: *Klicke darauf.* Jetzt kannst du die Birne über die App steuern: *ein- und ausschalten, sogar die Farbe wechseln.*
Oma: Vielen Dank!

4 Check your listening skills

Rob: I think I'll get a pair of these jeans. I like the advert. The *design is simple* and *the message is that* the jeans are just comfortable and easy.
Nell: *The advert appeals to people* who want basic clothes, not luxury.
Rob: Right, that's what I like. And the advert *addresses concerns about the environment*: it says that the jeans are made from organic cotton.
Nell: I think that you're exactly *their target audience*!

Unit 4 p. 53, p. 54

1 Check your vocabulary

1 There is a huge *contrast* between the lives of the very rich and the very poor.
2 The *literacy* rate in India is lower among women than among men.
3 Discrimination against lower *castes* is illegal in India, but still happens.
4 More people from lower castes have been put into government jobs by *quotas*.
5 I have a lot of things *delivered* because I don't have time to go shopping.
6 Putting rubbish and waste in rivers *pollutes* the water.
7 I wish you wouldn't *interrupt* me all the time.
8 He reads his *horoscope* every day, although he doesn't really believe in it.
9 We were *thrilled* to see our photos in the newspaper.
10 They took an autorickshaw around Agra, looking at the *architecture*.

2 Check your language

a This film (1) *was made* about 10 years ago. It (2) *is / has been included* in a lot of "Best films of all time" lists. The star (3) *hadn't been offered* a role in it, but he asked the director to let him try out for the lead role. The film (4) *is set* in a small Indian village in the 19th century. It (5) *will / is going to be shown* on TV later tonight and I think it (6) *will be watched* by a lot of people. Our teacher said it (7) *should be seen* by anyone who doesn't already know it.

b 1 Can seats be reserved? – Yes, *seats can be reserved*.
2 Will the platform number be shown on the board? – Yes, *it will be shown on the board*.
3 Is food served on the train? – Yes, *food is served on the train*.
4 *Were the tickets booked* online? – No, the tickets were booked here at the train station.
5 *Have the tickets been paid for / Were the tickets paid for*? – Yes, the tickets were paid for when they were booked.

3 Check your writing

Dear Mathilda

In your email you mentioned that you would be interested in riding an elephant in India, so I wanted to give you *my opinion* of this activity.

There is a lot of discussion about elephant riding. Some tourists have seen images of people riding elephants and have this experience on their must-do lists for India. *In my view*, riding an elephant isn't a good idea. They are *said to be* taken from their mothers as babies and you can see that they are often treated badly. Some places offering elephant rides now call themselves rescue centres, but I *don't believe* that the elephants are treated any better there than in other places. *By the* way, some animal rights groups are trying to get elephant rides banned (like circuses with animals in Germany and the US), so you might not be allowed to ride one anyhow.

While it's necessary to support India's tourism industry, *it's* also *important* to protect animals! I *agree* that riding elephants could be a fun experience, but I *strongly believe* that it's wrong to do it.

Yours

Nagesh

4 Check your mediation skills

1 Eine Gruppe schöner Tempel, Gärten und Paläste.
2 Man wird am Hotel abgeholt und mit einem privaten Wagen zur Festung gebracht.
3 Der/Die Reiseführer/in zeigt bei einem Spaziergang die tolle Architektur und fabelhaften Aussichten. Man besichtigt Hawa Mahal und erfährt etwas über die Geschichte der Festung.
4 Online oder per Telefon, mindestens zwei Tage vorher.
5 Nein, man kann sie auch auf dem Smartphone zeigen.
6 Wenn man es mindestens drei Tage vor der Führung macht.

Spelling p. 15

1 LISTENING Understanding the spoken alphabet

1	*D*	4	*K*	7	*U*	10	*M*	13	*C*
2	*X*	5	*V*	8	*J*	11	*B*	14	*R*
3	*A*	6	*C*	9	*W*	12	*E*	15	*Y*

2 Spelling words

a

	Name	City	Code
1	*Chloe*	*Sydney*	*ZM453*
2	*Harper*	*Melbourne*	*YS891*
3	*Joshua*	*Adelaide*	*QP276*
4	*Koen*	*Brisbane*	*WV402*

3 SPEAKING A phone call

a **Partner A**

Name of student: *Alex Winter*
Email address: *alex-winter@example.com*
Phone number: *+49 (0)162 2082784*

Partner B

Flight: *WXY 2993*
Leaves at: *9.35 am* Arrives: *next day at 3 pm*
Spoke to: *Kim Meyer*

Charts and statistics p. 16

1 Numbers and statistics

1 The number of people in Australia:
in 1901: 4,000,000 in 2018: *25,000,000*

2 The median age of Australians was twenty-two point five in 1901. In 2018, it was *thirty-seven point two*.

3 In 1901, the ratio of males *to* females was 110 *to* 100. In 2018, the ratio of males *to females was 98 to 100*.

4 In 1901, thirty-seven *point two* per cent of Australians lived in a state capital. In 2018, it was *sixty-seven point one* or a little over *two-thirds*.

2 REVISION Talking about charts and diagrams

a **Partner A**

1 (A) How many Australian citizens were born *in India*?
2 (A) *Where* were 167,000 Australian citizens born?
3 (B) What do a little less than *(fraction)* *a third* of Australians give as their religion?
4 (B) What *percentage* of Australians are Hindu?

Partner B

1 (A) *How many* Australian citizens were born in England?
2 (A) Where were 185,000 *Australian citizens born*?
3 (B) What percentage of Australians belong to *Islam*?
4 (B) Which religion do a little more than (*fraction*) *half* of Australians belong to?

b Partner A

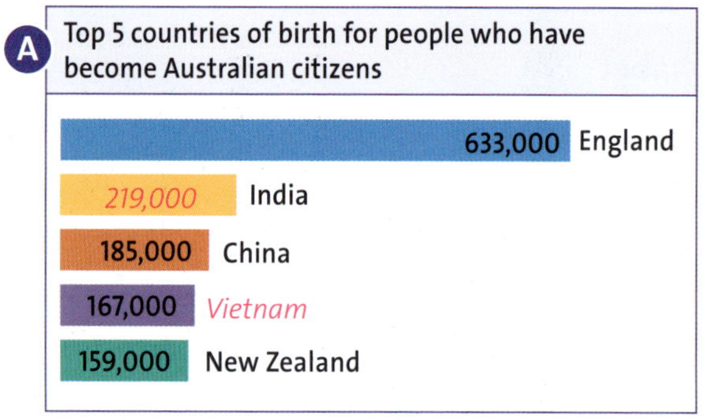

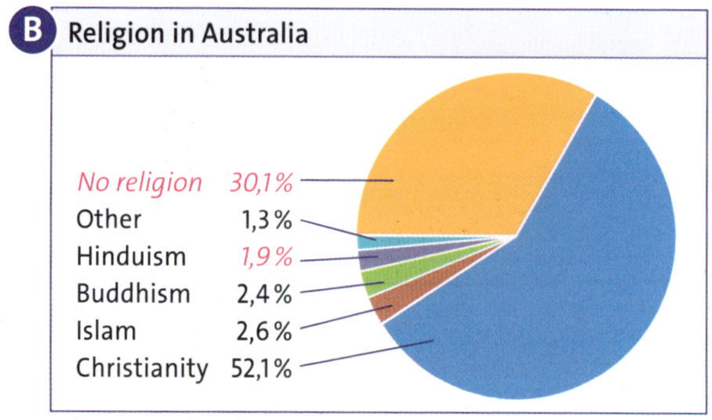

Partner B

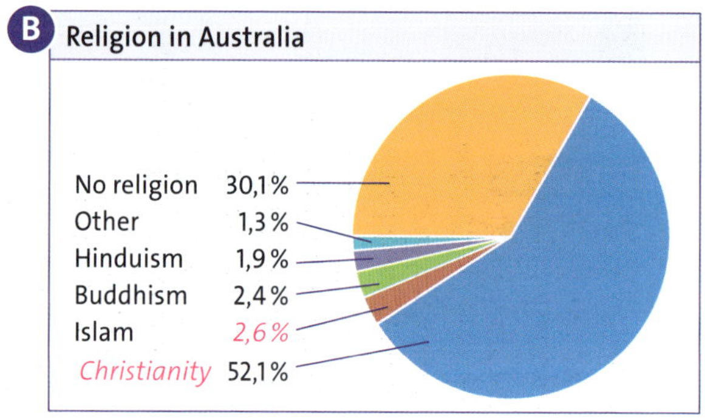

Source charts A and B: Based on ABS, Census of Population and Housing 2016

Aktiv

Zeiten	Bildung	Beispiel	Verneinung	Frage
Simple present	Infinitiv (+ *-s/-es* bei *he/she/it*)	I play golf. He plays golf.	I don't play golf. He doesn't play golf.	Do you play golf? Does he play golf?
Present progressive	Form von *be* + Infinitiv + *-ing*	I am playing golf. She is playing golf.	I'm not playing golf. She isn't playing golf.	Are you playing golf? Is he playing golf?
Simple past	Infinitiv + *-ed* oder unregelmäßige Formen	I played golf. He played golf.	I didn't play golf. He didn't play golf.	Did you play golf? Did he play golf?
Past progressive	Vergangenheit von *be* + Infinitiv + *-ing*	I was playing golf. She was playing golf.	I wasn't playing golf. She wasn't playing golf.	Were you playing golf? Was she playing golf?
Present perfect	*have/has* + past participle	I have played golf. He has played golf.	I haven't played golf. He hasn't played golf.	Have you played golf? Has he played golf?
Present perfect progressive	*have/has been* + Infinitiv + *-ing*	I have been playing golf. She has been playing golf.	I haven't been playing golf. She hasn't been playing golf.	Have you been playing golf? Has she been playing golf?
Past perfect	*had* + past participle	I had played golf. He had played golf.	I hadn't played golf. He hadn't played golf.	Had you played golf? Had he played golf?
***Will*-future**	*will* + Infinitiv	I will play golf. She will play golf.	I won't play golf. She won't play golf.	Will you play golf? Will she play golf?
***Going to*-future**	Form von *be* + *going to* + Infinitiv	I am going to play golf. He is going to play golf.	I'm not going to play golf. He isn't going to play golf.	Are you going to play golf? Is he going to play golf?

Passiv

Zeiten	Bildung	Beispiel	Verneinung	Frage
Simple present	Form von *be* + past participle	It is shown on TV. They are shown on TV.	It isn't shown on TV. They aren't shown on TV.	Is it shown on TV? Are they shown on TV?
Simple past	Vergangenheit von *be* + past participle	It was shown on TV. They were shown on TV.	It wasn't shown on TV. They weren't shown on TV.	Was it shown on TV? Were they shown on TV?
Present perfect	*have/has* + *been* + past participle	It has been shown on TV. They have been shown on TV.	It hasn't been shown on TV. They haven't been shown on TV.	Has it been shown on TV? Have they been shown on TV?
Past perfect	*had* + *been* + past participle	It had been shown on TV. They had been shown on TV.	It hadn't been shown on TV. They hadn't been shown on TV.	Had it been shown on TV? Had they been shown on TV?
***Will*-future**	*will* + *be* + past participle	It will be shown on TV. They will be shown on TV.	It won't be shown on TV. They won't be shown on TV.	Will it be shown on TV? Will they be shown on TV?
***Going to*-future**	Form von *be* + *going to* + *be* + past participle	It is going to be shown on TV. They are going to be shown on TV.	It isn't going to be shown on TV. They aren't going to be shown on TV.	Is it going to be shown on TV? Are they going to be shown on TV?
Modals	*can/must/...* + *be* + past participle	It can be shown on TV. They must be shown on TV.	It can't be shown on TV. They mustn't be shown on TV.	Can it be shown on TV? Must they be shown on TV?

Irregular verbs

infinitive	simple past	past participle	*Bedeutung*
(to) **be**	I/he/she/it **was**; you/we/you/they **were**	**been**	sein
(to) **bear**	**bore**	**borne**	ertragen, aushalten; tragen
(to) **beat**	**beat**	**beaten**	schlagen, besiegen
(to) **become**	**became**	**become**	werden
(to) **begin**	**began**	**begun**	anfangen, beginnen
(to) **bite**	**bit**	**bitten**	beißen; stechen *(z. B. Insekten)*
(to) **bleed**	**bled**	**bled**	bluten
(to) **blow**	**blew** [uː]	**blown**	pusten, blasen; wehen
(to) **break** [eɪ]	**broke**	**broken**	brechen
(to) **bring**	**brought**	**brought**	bringen, mitbringen
(to) **build** [ɪ]	**built** [ɪ]	**built** [ɪ]	bauen
(to) **burn**	**burnt**	**burnt**	brennen, verbrennen
(to) **burst**	**burst**	**burst**	brechen, bersten, platzen
(to) **buy**	**bought**	**bought**	kaufen
(to) **catch**	**caught**	**caught**	(ein)fangen; erwischen
(to) **choose**	**chose**	**chosen**	wählen, auswählen
(to) **come**	**came**	**come**	kommen
(to) **cost**	**cost**	**cost**	kosten
(to) **cut**	**cut**	**cut**	schneiden; *(Rasen)* mähen
(to) **deal (with)**	**dealt**	**dealt**	sich kümmern (um); sich befassen (mit), behandeln *(z. B. Thema)*
(to) **do**	**did**	**done** [ʌ]	tun, machen
(to) **dig**	**dug**	**dug**	graben
(to) **draw**	**drew**	**drawn**	zeichnen
(to) **drink**	**drank**	**drunk**	trinken
(to) **drive** [aɪ]	**drove** [əʊ]	**driven** [ɪ]	fahren
(to) **eat** [iː]	**ate** [et, eɪt]	**eaten** [iː]	essen
(to) **fall**	**fell**	**fallen**	fallen
(to) **feed**	**fed**	**fed**	füttern
(to) **feel**	**felt**	**felt**	fühlen, sich fühlen
(to) **fight**	**fought**	**fought**	kämpfen, bekämpfen
(to) **find**	**found**	**found**	finden
(to) **fly**	**flew**	**flown**	fliegen
(to) **forget**	**forgot**	**forgotten**	vergessen
(to) **freeze**	**froze**	**frozen**	(ge)frieren; erstarren
(to) **get**	**got**	**got**	bekommen; (sich etw.) besorgen, holen
(to) **give** [ɪ]	**gave**	**given** [ɪ]	geben
(to) **go**	**went**	**gone**	gehen, fahren
(to) **grow**	**grew**	**grown**	anbauen; werden; wachsen
(to) **hang**	**hung** [ʌ]	**hung**	hängen
(to) **have**	**had**	**had**	haben
(to) **hear** [ɪə]	**heard** [ɜː]	**heard**	hören
(to) **hide**	**hid**	**hidden**	(sich) verstecken
(to) **hit**	**hit**	**hit**	treffen auf, schlagen, prallen, stoßen
(to) **hold**	**held**	**held**	halten
(to) **hurt**	**hurt**	**hurt**	verletzen; wehtun
(to) **keep**	**kept**	**kept**	(be)halten
(to) **kneel**	**knelt**	**knelt**	knien
(to) **know** [nəʊ]	**knew** [njuː]	**known** [nəʊn]	wissen; kennen
(to) **lead**	**led**	**led**	führen, leiten
(to) **leave**	**left**	**left**	lassen, zurücklassen, verlassen
(to) **lend**	**lent**	**lent**	(ver)leihen

infinitive	simple past	past participle	*Bedeutung*
(to) let	let	let	lassen
(to) light	lit	lit	anzünden
(to) lose [uː]	lost	lost	verlieren
(to) make	made	made	machen, herstellen
(to) mean [iː]	meant [e]	meant [e]	bedeuten; sagen wollen
(to) meet	met	met	treffen
(to) pay	paid	paid	(be)zahlen
(to) put	put	put	legen, stellen, stecken
(to) read [iː]	read [e]	read [e]	lesen
(to) reset	reset	reset	zurücksetzen; resetten
°(to) rewrite	rewrote	rewritten	neu schreiben, umschreiben
(to) ride [aɪ]	rode	ridden [ɪ]	reiten; *(Rad)* fahren
(to) ring	rang	rung	läuten, klingeln
(to) rise	rose	risen	(an)steigen; sich erheben
(to) run	ran	run	rennen, laufen
(to) say	said [sed]	said [sed]	sagen
(to) see	saw	seen	sehen
°(to) seek	sought	sought	suchen
(to) sell	sold	sold	verkaufen
(to) send	sent	sent	senden, schicken
(to) set	set	set	stellen, legen, setzen
(to) sew	sewed	sewn	nähen
(to) shake	shook	shaken	schütteln
(to) shoot	shot	shot	(er)schießen
(to) show	showed	shown	zeigen
(to) shut	shut	shut	(ver)schließen
(to) sing	sang	sung	singen
(to) sit	sat	sat	sitzen; sich setzen
(to) sleep	slept	slept	schlafen
°(to) slide	slid	slid	schieben, gleiten (lassen)
(to) speak [iː]	spoke	spoken	sprechen
(to) speed	sped	sped	rasen, zu schnell fahren
(to) spend	spent	spent	*(Geld)* ausgeben, *(Zeit)* verbringen
(to) spin	spun	spun	(sich) drehen
(to) spread	spread	spread	verbreiten, sich ausbreiten
(to) stand	stood	stood	stehen
(to) steal	stole	stolen	stehlen, rauben
°(to) stick	stuck	stuck	kleben
(to) sting	stung	stung	stechen *(Insekt)*; brennen
(to) sweep	swept	swept	fegen, kehren
(to) swim	swam	swum	schwimmen
(to) swing	swung	swung	schwingen
(to) take	took	taken	(mit)nehmen; bringen
(to) teach [iː]	taught [ɔː]	taught [ɔː]	lehren, unterrichten
(to) tell	told	told	sagen; erzählen, berichten
(to) think	thought	thought	denken, glauben, meinen
(to) throw	threw	thrown	werfen
(to) understand	understood	understood	verstehen
(to) wake up	woke up	woken up	aufwachen; (auf)wecken
(to) wear [eə]	wore [ɔː]	worn [ɔː]	tragen *(Kleidung)*
(to) win	won [ʌ]	won [ʌ]	gewinnen
(to) write [aɪ]	wrote	written [ɪ]	schreiben

°Mit diesem Kringel sind Wörter markiert, die nicht zum Lernwortschatz gehören.

Quellenverzeichnis

Titelbild

Shutterstock.com/totajla

Illustrationen

Karen Donnelly: **S. 19**; **S. 23**; **S. 26**; **S. 33**; **S. 34**; **S. 35**

Bilder

S. 3 oben: stock.adobe.com/Katsiaryna, Mitte: Shutterstock.com/Bernhard Richter, unten: stock.adobe.com/rrudenkois; **S. 6**: bpk/DeA Picture Library/N. Cirani; **S. 7**: Shutterstock.com/THPStock; **S. 8** oben: Shutterstock.com/Kristian Bell, Mitte: mauritius images/Prisma, unten: Shutterstock.com/Ken Griffiths; **S. 9**: Shutterstock.com/THPStock; **S. 10**: dpa Picture-Alliance/AP Photo; **S. 11**: Shutterstock.com/Lukas Gojda; **S. 12** bushwalking: Shutterstock.com/Leah-Anne Thompson, cricket: Shutterstock.com/ChrisVanLennepPhoto, frisbee: Shutterstock.com/l i g h t p o e t, netball: Panther Media GmbH/Chris DeSilver, rock climbing: Shutterstock.com/Sergey Novikov, sailing: mauritius images/alamy stock photo/Ashley Cooper pics, snorkelling: Shutterstock.com/onlyjayne, surfing: stock.adobe.com/Thomas Sztanek; **S. 13** li.: Shutterstock.com/superjoseph, re. Emoticon: Shutterstock.com/AmazeinDesign; **S. 14**: Shutterstock.com/len4ik; **S. 17** li.: Shutterstock.com/SpeedKingz, re.: Shutterstock.com/Dmytro Zinkevych; **S. 18**: Shutterstock.com/Helga Potter; **S. 21**: Shutterstock.com/Dori Arwandi; **S. 25**: Shutterstock.com/iurii; **S. 27**: Shutterstock.com/Hrecheniuk Oleksii; **S. 29** oben: iRony/Radheya Jegatheva/interfilm Berlin Management GmbH; **S. 30**: Shutterstock.com/Burdun Iliya; **S. 32**: Shutterstock.com/pashabo; **S. 37**: ClipDealer GmbH/SeanPrior; **S. 38**: Shutterstock.com/KOBRIN PHOTO; **S. 40** oben: Shutterstock.com/Mile Atanasov, unten: Shutterstock.com/Prostock-studio; **S. 41** li.: Shutterstock.com/Barabasa, re.: Shutterstock.com/Syda Productions; **S. 43** Bild A: mauritius images/alamy stock photo/Visuals Stock, Bild B: Shutterstock.com/Milica Nistoran, Bild C: Shutterstock.com/Lalam photography, Bild D: Shutterstock.com/Dinesh Hukmani, Bild E: mauritius images/alamy stock photo/Dorling Kindersley ltd; Bild F: Shutterstock.com/Abhishek Bagrodia; **S. 45**: Shutterstock.com/Rob Marmion; **S. 46** oben: Picturetime Digiplex Pvt Ltd., unten: Shutterstock.com/mikumistock; **S. 47**: mauritius images/alamy stock photo/dbimages; **S. 49**: mauritius images/alamy stock photo/Richard Splash; **S. 51**: Shutterstock.com/saiko3p; **S. 54**: Shutterstock.com/nicepix; **S. 57** li.: Shutterstock.com/SpeedKingz, re.: Shutterstock.com/Dmytro Zinkevych; **S. 58**: Shutterstock.com/antoniodiaz; **S. 59**: Shutterstock.com/antoniodiaz; **S. 60** li.: Shutterstock.com/Tero Vesalainen, re.: Shutterstock.com/Rocketclips, Inc.; **S. 61** li.: Shutterstock.com/superjoseph, re. Emoticon: Shutterstock.com/AmazeinDesign

Text

S. 29 *Twitter kills prose* (...): iRony/Radheya Jegatheva/interfilm Berlin Management GmbH